FIRE
CATASTROPHES

C_E

FIRE
CATASTROPHES

HENRY RUSSELL

ISBN 0-86288-159-5

Printed and bound in Italy

For Brown Partworks Ltd

Editor: Shona Grimbly
Design: Wilson Design Associates
Picture research: Wendy Verren
Production: Alex MacKenzie

Page 1: *The Great Fire of London burned for three days in September 1666 and destroyed most of the City of London.*

Pages 2-3: *On November 20, 1992, fire broke out in the English royal residence of Windsor Castle and raged for seven hours, wrecking many of the historic state apartments.*

Below right: *The two miners who were rescued after being trapped for seven days below ground when fire broke out in the Sunshine mine at Kellogg, USA.*

CONTENTS

INTRODUCTION 6

CHAPTER 1
THE GREATEST OF
THEM ALL 12

CHAPTER 2
WAR AND CRIME 30

CHAPTER 3
PUBLIC PLACES 50

CHAPTER 4
UNDERGROUND FIRES 90

CHAPTER 5
INDUSTRIAL FIRES 106

INDEX 128

INTRODUCTION

As a rule most of the famous fires in history have been caused by carelessness, bad luck, or a combination of both – a chance spark from a piece of machinery that happened to land on some highly flammable substance (Düsseldorf airport, 1996), a small fire in a kitchen that quickly flared out of control and engulfed a whole building (the Grand Hotel, Las Vegas, 1980), a carelessly discarded cigarette end or match that smoldered and then burst into a raging inferno (the Sennichi Building, Osaka, 1972). Time and again, trivial incidents such as these have mushroomed into headline-making catastrophes that have claimed hundreds – or thousands – of lives.

Right: The Great Fire of Chicago broke out on October 8, 1871, and burned for nearly three days. The flames were so intense that they leaped over the Chicago River, destroying all in their path.

Above: A view of San Francisco and the fire that followed the earthquake in April 1906. The center of the city was almost totally destroyed, and over 200,000 people were left without homes.

Malice and deliberate action also play their parts, of course, but generally their roles are minor. It is most often chance that sets in motion a disastrous chain of events. Even those who start fires deliberately seldom have any clear preconception of the extent of the destruction that may eventually be caused by their deeds. John "Gypsy" Thompson – who firebombed an after-hours club in London in 1980 because he thought he had been overcharged for a drink – no doubt had murder in mind, but he probably did not realize he would kill 37 people.

US President Franklin D. Roosevelt and his chiefs of staff, who masterminded the 1945 Tokyo firebombing massacre, most likely did not foresee that their actions would lead to the deaths of 200,000 people. What they certainly did not anticipate was that the bombing would redouble Japanese determination to fight on to the bitter end of World War II.

Many of the worst fires occur in public places, often through the malfunction or complete absence of safety equipment. At Club Cinq-Sept in Grenoble, France, in

1970, there were no fire extinguishers, and not even a phone from which to call for help. As a result of this 146 people died.

The 50 people who died in the 1973 fire at the Summerland holiday complex in the Isle of Man would not have been killed if the overall roof had not been made of a widely banned acrylic sheeting that melted and turned the building into a gas oven full of raining liquid plastic.

Some fires are the product of false economies or of wrong-headed ideas about what is safe. After reading the account of the 1974 fire at the Joelma Building in São Paulo, it may be difficult to credit that a skyscraper without a helicopter landing pad on its roof could ever have been built higher than the furthest extension of the fire brigade's ladders.

What is abundantly clear from these case histories is that whether a fire is started by accident or by arson or an act of war, inadequate safety precautions – or a complete lack of them – can turn a small fire into a major catastrophe.

Right: The fire at Bradford City football stadium in England. A total of 56 people were burned to death when a timber stand caught fire on May 11, 1985.

Below: In Philadelphia, USA, fire swept through a residential district when police bombed the headquarters of Move, an "anti-society" radical organization.

One of the most destructive fires in terms of lives lost took place in 1982 during the Afghan War (1979-1989), but it was as bad as it was mainly because of a misunderstanding. Russian troops guarding a tunnel thought the noise they heard was an enemy attack, and immediately shut both ends of it as a "safety" measure. Only when it was too late did they realize that by doing so they had trapped more than a thousand of their comrades-in-arms in a cloud of poisonous gas from an oil fire inside the tunnel.

Most great fires start suddenly, do their work quickly, and are over not very long afterwards. It is usually the case that people who happen to be in the wrong place at the wrong time are those who are killed. When a fire gets going, it destroys everyone and everything in its path.

If this book contains a message, it is that people can do little to avoid being caught in a fire beyond carrying on with their normal lives and trusting to luck. There are no reasonable precautions that anyone can take to protect themselves from a violent killer that may strike anywhere, any time.

Or perhaps there is something one can do. Anyone visiting a hotel, nightclub, cinema, or theater should check where the nearest fire exit is, and also check that it is unlocked. If it is locked, complain to the management and leave at once. A sickening number of fire catastrophes have happened when people in public

Above: In March 1986 a fire in England's historic Hampton Court Palace killed one elderly resident and destroyed much of the 17th-century south wing.

Right: Firemen fighting the blaze at the Sandoz chemical factory in Basel, Switzerland, in November 1986.

Right: The remains of a scorched forest in Ukhta, Russia, after a gas pipeline ignited in April, 1995, causing a blaze that ravaged the area.

buildings have been unable to get out – because the management had locked the fire exits to prevent people getting in or leaving without paying.

Fires in the workplace have also taken a high toll of life. The most destructive of these have been in under-

ground mines. Here, there are great dangers anyway, but the risks have often been increased by inadequate safety precautions. But it is not necessarily safer to be employed above ground. Many of the 125 who died high up in the New York Triangle Waist building in 1911 would probably have survived if the owners of the factory had not been in the habit of locking the workrooms to ensure that their employees didn't leave work early.

There is very seldom enough or indeed any warning of a fire disaster: North Sea oil riggers on Piper Alpha in 1988 were unaware of any problem until they heard the banshee-like squeal of escaping gas just 30 seconds before the first explosion. One exception was the 1987 fire at King's Cross Underground rail station in London. For hours before the catastrophe, passengers had seen smoke coming from cracks in the escalator. Station staff were notified but did nothing, perhaps because they did not take the warnings seriously, or perhaps because they had received no training in what to do in the event of fire. Later that evening, a fireball erupted from the foot of the moving staircase and killed 30 people in the station concourse.

The destructive power of fire is so great that it often destroys important evidence that might have shown what caused it. People who have witnessed this power at close quarters are unanimous about one thing – fire should be feared. Everyone in charge of public places and buildings where large numbers of people congregate should be constantly alert to this danger.

Above: A Malaysian fireman uses a tree branch to fight the forest fires that rampaged throughout Southeast Asia during the autumn of 1997.

Right: On the night of January 30, 1996, fire devastated Venice's famous opera house, La Fenice.

THE GREATEST
OF THEM ALL

In addition to being among the worst in history, the fires in this chapter are among the best known. The reasons for their notoriety vary, as do their causes, but what they have in common is that they are the disasters that people first call to mind whenever great fires are mentioned.

All but one of them broke out accidentally – the single exception is the 1933 Reichstag fire in Berlin which was started by the Nazis in order to discredit their political opponents. The fire itself was not remarkable, but its political consequences were cataclysmic and affected most of the world for the next 12 years.

The great fires of Tokyo and San Francisco were caused indirectly by earthquakes. No one really knows what caused the Great Fire of Chicago – all that can be said is that, for as long as it remained built of wood, the city was particularly susceptible to fire and the ashes of lesser Chicago infernos blow through several other pages of this book.

The odd one out is the fire in a church in Chile – when it happened, in 1863, there was scant coverage in European newspapers of South American affairs, and thus it never became engraved on the general consciousness in the same way as the Great Fires of Rome and London. But the destruction of La Compania in Santiago remains to this day the fire that killed the most people in a single building.

Right: Bush fires in February 1983 in South Australia spread out of control, destroying everything in their path and killing 68 people. Because the fires began at the beginning of Lent, the disaster was called Ash Wednesday.

ROME

JULY 18, AD 64

Left: The Emperor Nero watching Rome burn. At the time Nero was generally believed to have started the fire himself. The contemporary historian Suetonius reported that Nero "set the city on fire so openly that his attendants were caught with burning torches in their hands."

The Great Fire of Rome is one of the earliest fire disasters in history about which there is reliable documentary evidence. Although details are scarce – neither the number of deaths nor the full extent of the damage to property has ever been accurately determined – the fire is known to have been a wide-ranging and cataclysmic inferno with important consequences for the city and its people.

Fire had long been one of the greatest hazards in the tightly-packed wooden houses of ancient Rome, and had caused extensive damage at various times in its history. The first Roman Emperor, Augustus Caesar, who ruled from 27 BC to AD 14, made fire prevention one of his top priorities. In 21 BC, he organized the first Roman fire brigade, a band of irregulars comprised of slaves under the command of officials who until then had been in charge of streets and markets. This did not solve the problem, however, and after a bad fire in AD 6 Augustus established the first corps of professional firemen – known in Latin as *vigiles* – made up of seven squads or cohorts of 1000 freemen each.

The Great Fire broke out on the bright moonlit night of July 18, AD 64, and raged unchecked for over a week, totally destroying three of Rome's 14 regions and partially destroying seven others. Then, as now, it was commonly believed that the fire had been started by the Emperor Nero (who ruled from AD 54 to 68). He was away from Rome at the time, and his alibi seemed suspiciously convenient.

Alarmed that the population seemed to be blaming him, Nero tried to blame the fire on the Jews. Although the Emperor's second wife, Poppaea Sabina, maintained that they were innocent, the Jews were widely persecuted in the aftermath of the blaze. The most famous victims of the ensuing violence were Saints Peter and Paul. Although by this time the Roman people were starting to differentiate between Jews and Christians, these two were not different enough to escape martyrdom. The climate of hatred and retribution created by the Fire continued into AD 65 – Nero remained unpopular, and when a plot to assassinate him was uncovered, the poet Lucan and numerous senators were executed.

Above: Nero amid the ruins of Rome. Nero took measures to control the fire and to find shelter for the homeless.

Above: After the Great Fire that destroyed most of Rome Nero punished those he held to be responsible.

However, no historian now believes that Nero was responsible in any way for the fire. Nor, indeed – contrary to popular legend – did the Emperor fiddle while Rome burned. The truth of the matter seems to have been that, on hearing the news from his capital, Nero rushed back and took strenuous measures to bring the fire under control and to supervise the provision of shelter for the homeless. Afterwards, Nero's initiatives to rebuild the city with broad thoroughfares acting as firebreaks contributed in no small measure to the modern-day appearance of Rome. Nevertheless, there were several other major fires in Rome, most notably in AD 80 during the reign of the Emperor Titus, when the Capitol, the Pantheon, and Agrippa's Baths were among the buildings destroyed.

THE GREAT FIRE OF LONDON

SEPTEMBER 2–5, 1666

Below: People took to the river in an attempt to escape the flames.

Bottom: The fire as seen from the south bank of the River Thames.

The Great Fire of London was the worst fire in the city's history. It destroyed a large part of the City of London, including most of the civic buildings, old St Paul's Cathedral, 87 parish churches and about 13,000 houses. At least nine people were burned to death. Some important historical insights into this appalling disaster are contained in the diaries of Samuel Pepys (1633–1703), who was living in London at the time.

The fire broke out accidentally at King Charles II's baker in Pudding Lane near London Bridge when a spark from the ovens ignited the hay in a neighboring inn yard. The blaze spread quickly, partly because of the density of the surrounding wooden buildings, and partly because so many of them were full of combustible matter such as pitch and tar, oil and brandy. By the following morning, half a mile of the River Thames waterfront was ablaze.

It was the end of summer and the weather had been hot and dry for some time. According to Pepys, this made "everything, after so long a drought . . . combustible, even the very stones of churches." A strong east wind fanned the flames, which raged during the rest of Monday and part of Tuesday.

At first, people tried to save their possessions as well as their lives. Some loaded up horses and carts full of their belongings and set off to the fields of Hampstead and Highgate; others moved their belongings from one burning house to another still unaffected nearby. But their efforts were futile: the fire was rampant and took all before it. Soon the Thames was swarming with barges full of people who by now were taking with them only what they were able to carry. Even on the water, however, they were not entirely safe: the conflagration was now so strong that, as Pepys describes it, "with one's face in the wind, you were almost burned with showers of firedrops."

Pepys and others advised the King to blow up the houses in the fire's path to create a firebreak, but the conflagration outran them. Sir Thomas Bloodworth,

Southwarke

Lord Mayor of London, lamented: "What can I do? I have been pulling down houses. But the fire overtakes us faster than we can do it."

On Wednesday the fire slackened and began to burn itself out; on Thursday it was largely extinguished, but in the evening of that day the flames again burst forth in the Temple, one of the Inns of Court. Some houses in Tower Street, next to the Tower of London, were at once blown up by gunpowder and after that it became easy to quench what fire remained. The fire was finally mastered.

Within a few days of the fire, King Charles II was presented with three different proposals for the reconstruction of the city – two were drawn up by the architects Christopher Wren and John Evelyn, and the other by the city's Surveyor of Works, Robert Hooke. Although they all contained plans to regularize the streets, none was adopted and nearly all the old thoroughfares were retained. Nevertheless, Wren's greatest achievement, the new St Paul's Cathedral, did get built and still stands today.

Below: The devastation caused by the fire in the city of timber-framed houses was horrifying. When the city was rebuilt, less combustible materials were used, such as brick and stone.

Above: Fanned by a strong east wind the flames spread rapidly through the close-packed streets of wooden houses. The terrified Londoners were able to snatch up only a few possessions as they fled in fear of their lives

LA COMPANIA CHURCH, SANTIAGO, CHILE

DECEMBER 8, 1863

Below: The city of Santiago, capital of Chile, with the Andes mountains behind it. Here, one of the worst ever fire disasters happened in the Church of La Campania.

In the world's worst fire disaster in a single building, approximately 2500 people – nearly all women and children – were burned to death as flames spread quickly through La Compania church in Santiago, the capital of Chile. That there were very few men among the victims is explained by the fact that the tragedy occurred on the Feast of the Immaculate Conception. This day – one of the most important dates in the Roman Catholic calendar – is of particular significance to women because it celebrates the doctrine that Mary, the mother of Jesus, was preserved from original sin.

The interior of the 17th-century La Compania church – famously beautiful in itself – had been specially decorated for the occasion with colored lamps which had been hung in groups in every nook and cranny of the building. The parishioners were keen to celebrate the festival as memorably as they could, while the parish priests are thought to have been annoyed by remarks attributed to a Papal Nuncio, who compared the Chileans' religious celebrations unfavourably with those in Rome. One local priest, Father Ugarto, was particularly annoyed by adverse criticisms of the lighting in Chilean churches: he is reputed to have

Above: The ruins of the 17th-century Church of La Campania after the fire. The church could hold 3000 people, and it was full to capacity on the Feast of the Immaculate Conception when the fire broke out.

responded with the words: "I will give the Nuncio such an illumination as the world has never seen."

As a consequence, on December 8, the day of the Feast, there were some 20,000 of these candle-powered lamps spread all around the interior of La Compania. Priests and lay helpers had spent several hours during the afternoon lighting them all in readiness for the evening service.

The service was due to begin at 1900 hours. At a couple of minutes before the hour, the church was full to capacity, with about 3000 people squatting on prayer mats – there were no chairs or pews. On the altar, the centrepiece of the service, was a statue of the Virgin Mary with her feet set upon a crescent moon made of canvas and wood: the moon flickered atmospherically from the light of the lamps inside it.

On the stroke of the hour, the moon at the feet of the Virgin Mary caught fire and flames spread quickly through the building. Only the main door was open and this was not large enough to let all the congregation out in time. The door of the other potential escape route, through the sacristy, had been shut by the priests behind them as they fled to safety. Chaos reigned as the congregation stampeded.

The church was completely gutted in less than 30 minutes. Of the victims, many were under 20 years old. The bereaved men of the city blamed the priests who they thought had made good their own escape and left the congregation to die.

THE GREAT CHICAGO FIRE, USA

OCTOBER 8–10, 1871

Four square miles of Chicago, including the whole of the business district, were destroyed in October 1871 by a blaze that raged across the city for nearly three days. The conditions were ideal for a fire – there had been a long, hot summer and most of the buildings were built of wood. Starting in a southwestern suburb, flames spread rapidly northeastward, leaping the Chicago River and dying out only when they reached Lake Michigan. About 250 people died, 90,000 more were made homeless, 18,000 buildings were destroyed and almost 200 million dollars' worth of property was lost.

Left: The Chicago fire was popularly supposed to have been started in a barn, when a cow kicked over a kerosene lamp which set fire to a pile of hay.

No one really knows how the Great Chicago Fire began, but according to popular legend it broke out in DeKoven Street, southwest Chicago, in a barn belonging to a woman called Mrs O'Leary. According to the story – which was always strenuously denied by the woman herself – at about 2100 hours on the night of October 8, her cow kicked over a lighted kerosene lamp which set fire to a pile of hay and wood shavings.

From there, the flames spread very quickly, fanned by a strong wind blowing from the west. The breeze pushed the fire away from the O'Learys' house – which miraculously emerged unscathed from the ensuing conflagration – and off in the direction of the downtown area. By midnight, the fire had reached the Chicago River. This should have been a natural barrier and the end of the matter, but the wind ferried blazing pieces of wood across the river and, once on the other

Left: Even the Chicago River could not stop the progress of the fire. The wind blew pieces of burning wood across the river to the other side where there was an abundance of combustible materials.

Right: The Chicago firemen fought the flames tirelessly, but with their limited resources they could not put out the conflagration.

side, the fire continued its progress toward the heart of the Midwest capital. Downtown there was an abundance of fuel – grain in great silos, lumber yards full of wood, coal depots and liquor distilleries. The fire services proved completely inadequate. There were only 17 horse-drawn fire engines and 23 hose carts, nowhere near enough to put out a fire of this size.

The *Chicago Daily Tribune* described how the flames would "hurl themselves bodily several hundred feet and kindle new buildings. The whole air was filled with glowing cinders, looking like an illuminated snowstorm. Fantastic fires of red, blue, and green played along the cornices of buildings."

The First National Bank building was popularly supposed to be fireproof and, although it did not catch light, it became so hot that its iron framework expanded until its external walls collapsed. In the downtown area, every hotel, every theater, and every bank was destroyed, together with the Grand Opera House and the City Hall. The fire only stopped when it reached the shores of Lake Michigan.

Despite the efforts of the citizens, the fire was never brought under control but simply exhausted itself. As the smoke cleared, the exhausted firefighters were amazed to see one house – the home of Mahlon Ogden – still largely intact amid a sea of ashes. The story is that, on seeing the flames approaching, the family soaked all their carpets, blankets, and sheets in water and hung them over the walls and roof, thus preventing their home from catching light.

SAN FRANCISCO FIRE, USA

APRIL 18–21, 1906

The earthquake that shattered San Francisco, California, USA at 0500 hours on the morning of Wednesday, April 18, 1906 was followed by a devastating fire that burned for four days and almost totally destroyed the city center.

What became a mighty inferno began as dozens of small fires scattered throughout the city. Some broke out from heaters left burning in buildings that had been abandoned during the earthquake. Others spread from hearths and kitchen ranges that had been overturned by the tremors. Many were triggered by severed electric cables or the ignition of gas from fractured gas pipes. Altogether, there were 52 of these small fires. Even in normal circumstances, the San Francisco Fire Department would have been hard pressed to cope with all of them at once because it had only 38 horse-drawn fire engines at its disposal. But these were not

Above: The devastation in the center of the city was almost total, leaving over 200,000 people homeless.

Left: People who managed to escape from the city watched the fire from the safety of Russian Hill.

Above: At the junction of Mission Street and Third Street rubble caused by the earthquake covers the ground while, in the background, the Opera House can be seen in flames.

normal circumstances – the city was already in chaos from the earthquake and great fissures in the streets had severed every water main. The only source of water for hoses was the Bay, and not all the fires were along the waterfront.

Fanned by a stiff breeze, the small fires came together in a great conflagration and by noon on the Wednesday it was out of control. Federal troops were called in, along with the National Guard and 600 helpers from the University of California at Berkeley on the other side of the Bay. They did not even try to put out the existing blaze – that was clearly impossible. Instead, they concentrated on saving as many lives as they could. They also dynamited buildings in an attempt to create an unbridgeable gap in the path of the advancing flames, but this turned out disastrously – the buildings blew outwards instead of collapsing and started new fires.

Looting became a serious problem. Martial law was imposed and the army was called in to help the overstretched police force. Mayor Schmitz sent out leaflets warning that thieves would be shot on sight, and at least three people were killed in this way.

By Saturday, the fires had begun to burn themselves out and rain helped to extinguish the last ones. Only then did the true scale of the disaster become clear – about 700 people had been killed, including 270 mental patients locked in their asylum who had burned to death. One man trapped inside a burning building persuaded a policeman to shoot him. City Hall was turned into a makeshift mortuary. More than 200,000 people were homeless and had to camp in tents in Golden Gate Park and other open spaces. Four square miles (10 sq km) of the city had been obliterated, including 514 blocks containing 28,000 buildings. The whole of Chinatown was reduced to ashes, as was all but one house in the fashionable Nob Hill residential district. Losses from the fire were 20 times greater than the losses from the earthquake and led to the largest ever fire insurance claim of 5,748 million dollars.

TOKYO AND YOKOHAMA, JAPAN

SEPTEMBER 2, 1923

One of the most destructive fires of all time broke out after three earthquakes in quick succession devastated the Japanese capital, Tokyo, and the neighbouring port of Yokohama, which lies eight miles (13km) to the southwest on Tokyo Bay.

The tremors, which were first felt in the morning at 1150 hours, quickly created huge chasms across the streets of both cities and many people were instantly swallowed up inside them. Overhead electricity cables and telephone wires snapped and fell onto passers-by who were immediately electrocuted. Underground gas mains were severed and then exploded, setting off fires which created even greater devastation.

Driven by strong winds, the flames soon engulfed the greater part of both city centers. In Tokyo, many people tried to find refuge in the open air – two of the most popular refuges were the grounds of the Imperial Palace and the shallow canals, where men, women, and children stood or were held for many hours in the hope that the fire would eventually exhaust itself.

But the flames were so strong that they were not impeded by water and many people were burned to death as they stood in the canals by whirling airborne sheets of flame. In Yokohama, the fire was further fuelled by explosions in the dockside oil tanks that had been ripped open by the earthquake.

The fire raged for 36 hours, and – although the army and the rescue services did their best – nothing could be done to impede its progress. In an effort to create a firebreak, unaffected buildings in its path were hastily

Below: Fire enveloped the center of Tokyo following the earthquake. Many people died in burning buildings and even in the open they were not safe from the flames.

demolished. Even this proved futile – either the explosions started new fires or the existing fire just jumped over the space before carrying on its way.

In the aftermath, although it was impossible to establish the cause of every death, it was generally agreed that the fire had killed more people than the earthquakes. Even the combined death toll remains unknown, but it is believed that no fewer than 150,000 people perished. A further 100,000 people were seriously injured.

The damage to property was so great that no one ever bothered to try and calculate it. At least 700,000 dwellings were destroyed – from the smallest houses to the largest hotels. In Tokyo, 17 libraries were burned

to the ground, including the Emperor's priceless collection, as well as 151 Shinto shrines, 633 Buddhist temples and numerous ornamental gardens.

In Yokohama – where the fire and the earthquake had been almost simultaneous – all the port buildings were destroyed, along with the American hospital and two large hotels. As the second and third shocks quickly followed, many people took to rowing boats and headed out into the Bay, where they thought they would be safer. But the flames pursued them even over the water. Although 12,000 people were picked up by the *Empress of Australia*, a liner docked at a safe distance from the shore, the death toll in Yokohama was at least 21,000.

Below: The shopping center of Tokyo suffered heavily in the earthquake and subsequent fire. Little remains of the Ginza, the "Street of Silver", so-called because of the amount of money that changed hands in the shops.

REICHSTAG, BERLIN, GERMANY

FEBRUARY 27, 1933

The political repercussions of the fire which largely destroyed the German parliament building were even greater than the conflagration itself. The German legislature was gutted during the night of February 27 by a fast-moving fire. The blaze was started deliberately – probably by someone setting a match to furniture piled on rugs inside the building – but at the time it was not clear who had done it. It is now known to have been the work of the ruling Nazis, who started the fire as a pretext for clamping down on opponents of their rule, particularly the communists, in the build-up to the elections of March 5.

Smoke was first noticed by a police officer on patrol in the Reichstag itself in the evening at about 2100 hours. The officer later claimed that, before raising the alarm, he had fired several shots at a group of men seen running away from the scene. He then managed to arrest one of them, a 24-year-old Dutchman named Marinus van der Lubbe, who – when searched – was found to be carrying a Communist Party membership card.

By the time the fire brigade arrived, the fire was well entrenched and had spread in many directions. The panelling, chairs, and desks of the Reichstag chamber were all made of wood and so burned easily.

The firemen fought bravely and brought the inferno under control before it reached the cupola. They also managed to save the library and reading room where countless priceless documents were stored.

Chancellor Adolf Hitler lost no time in linking the fire to the German left-wing and alleged a conspiracy:

Below: A fire engine stationed outside the Reichstag building as it burns on the night of February 27, 1933.

"Now you can see what Germany and Europe have to look for from Communism," he declared. He placed Hermann Göring, later to be head of the Luftwaffe, in charge of the investigation into the fire. Before dawn, police had arrested all 100 elected communist members of the Reichstag. They also rounded up other communists all over Berlin and detained them pending the outcome of the investigation at the scene.

The following evening, President von Hindenberg was persuaded to sign an emergency decree which suspended constitutional guarantees of individual freedom, freedom of the press, private property, and the secrecy of postal communications. Communist newspapers were shut down and suspected communist meeting places were closed.

This was originally supposed to have been a temporary measure, but it remained in force for 12 years: in that sense, the Reichstag fire marked the true beginning of the Nazi dictatorship.

Although Marinus van der Lubbe was mentally handicapped and almost certainly not the culprit, he was subsequently executed.

Above: The fire brigade tackling the blaze inside the Reichstag. It seems probable that the fire was set in several different places.

Right: Firemen surveying the damage to the interior of the Reichstag. They had managed to save the library and the reading room with their collections of priceless documents.

ASH WEDNESDAY, AUSTRALIA

FEBRUARY 16, 1983

I n many parts of Australia, bush fires are a recurring fact of life. But in February 1983 they became a multiple killer when 68 people died in a conflagration that spread across many parts of Victoria and South Australia. Adelaide, the South Australian capital, was covered by a pall of smoke blown in from other parts of the state. This happened at the start of Lent and as a result the tragedy became known as Ash Wednesday.

Ash Wednesday was not one fire but many fires which started at about the same time in different places and joined up to make one immense inferno. Most of them were accidental, an almost inevitable consequence of the heat and the dryness of the bush. Others, however, were started deliberately, and one 19-year-old man from Adelaide was later convicted of arson.

The fires broke out at the height of the summer, when temperatures were in the region of 100°F (38°C). South Australia was in the middle of its worst drought for a 100 years – many farmers there had not seen rain for more than 12 months and thousands of their sheep had had to be shot for lack of drinking water.

Once the flames started, the fires spread rapidly, fanned by northerly breezes which gusted at speeds of up to 50mph (80kph). Vast tracts of the two states were declared disaster areas with hundreds of homes destroyed and huge numbers of sheep and cattle burned to death. More than 20 people were killed in South Australia, most of them near Adelaide, while at least 10 others died in separate incidents in Victoria.

Police said that some of the victims had been trapped in cars as flames suddenly swept across a main road between Adelaide and the outlying hills. Twelve

Above: Fire-fighters were powerless to stem the blaze as strong winds fanned the flames into a terrifying conflagration.

firemen were killed, including three who died together in their truck as they were fighting one particular blaze. Ambulance services reported that 230 people in the southeast Adelaide region had been taken to hospital suffering from burns or from the effects of smoke inhalation. All soldiers in the area were called up for firefighting duties, but by the time they arrived many of the blazes raging through bush and eucalyptus trees were already out of control. Some people tried to save their homes by dousing their roofs with water, but the drought had necessitated water cuts and there was not enough water available for the purpose.

Melbourne airport had to be closed for 20 minutes as thick smoke swept in from fires to the south of the city. Residents in the Adelaide Hills suburb were forced to flee their wooden homes, dozens of which were destroyed by fire. One of the worst affected areas was around Lorne, 70 miles (112km) southwest of Melbourne. The coastal town was surrounded by fire and hundreds of people had to rush to the beach as flames swept out of the bush and into their homes. Four towns – Macedon, Melton, Riddell's Creek, and Woodend – in the Mount Macedon area about 50 miles (80km) northwest of Melbourne had to be evacuated.

Left: A householder inspects the remains of their home. Dozens of timber-built houses succumbed to the fire.

Right: A couple in front of their fire-ravaged house in Melbourne. The fires swept through much of South Australia, destroying everything in their path.

WAR AND CRIME

The fires in this chapter reflect man's inhumanity to man. They were all started during wartime, or as acts of terrorism during armed struggles against hostile authorities, or as criminal acts.

The firebomb attacks on Hamburg, Dresden, and Tokyo were part of a carefully thought out Allied strategy towards the end of World War II that aimed to demoralize the civilian populations of Germany and Japan. Although strategic targets of military importance were bombed in the first of these raids, during the last the bombers carried nothing but incendiary devices – they came with no other purpose than to start a fire that could not be controlled and that would have to be left to burn itself out. These missions were judged successful in terms of the destruction they caused, but their effect on the victims may well have been counter-productive.

The fires at the Abadan cinema, the London drinking clubs, and the Dublin dance hall illustrate both the ease with which a serious fire can be started and the unpredictability of its outcome. Although the Iranian terrorists clearly wanted to cause panic and probably death, they appear not to have known that the audience was locked in and would have little hope of escape or rescue.

Finally, it seems clear that the fire that destroyed La Fenice opera house in Venice was started deliberately in order to avoid financial loss. It was the work of a thoughtful arsonist who took great care to ensure that no one would get hurt.

Right: Venice's historic opera house, La Fenice, burns after being set on fire in January 1996. It was the second time in its history that the theater had suffered a major fire – in 1836 it burned to the ground but was rebuilt.

HAMBURG, GERMANY

JULY 25-28, 1943

At least 45,000 people were killed during a series of relentless attacks on Hamburg by bombers of the British RAF and the US Army Air Force (USAAF). Over 10,000 tons of explosives were dropped on Germany's second city, flattening an enormous area of it. Although strategically important targets such as factories, shipyards, and the tunnel under the River Elbe were destroyed, it was also part of the Allies' intention to terrorize the civilian population by creating firestorms.

A firestorm occurs when a fire becomes so intense that it uses up all the available oxygen in the air around it; then, as hot air rises, fresh oxygen is drawn down from above and replenishes the flames. This rapid movement of air also serves to fan the existing fires and temperatures may reach about 1800°F (1000°C). A firestorm is a terrifying phenomenon, and is virtually unstoppable by conventional firefighting forces.

Because of the intention to start a firestorm, the offensive was code-named "Operation Gomorrah", after the city destroyed by flame in the Old Testament.

The first raid of "Operation Gomorrah" began at about 0100 hours in the morning of Saturday, July 25, and was carried out by 791 RAF Lancaster, Stirling, Halifax, and Wellington bombers which approached central Hamburg from the east, flying in streams between the Alster Lakes and the Elbe. One of the areas worst affected by this attack was Billwerder near the railway marshalling yards – the fires that broke out there spread quickly north to the Hamm and Borgfelde residential neighborhoods.

Left: The devastation left by the bombing was appalling. Nevertheless, the citizens of Hamburg continued their daily lives as best they could.

Fire also consumed the densely populated old Altona, Hoheluft, and Eimsbüttel districts, where houses began to collapse and block the narrow streets. Soon St Pauli and the waterfront were also alight. Civilian casualties were particularly heavy, not only because of the intensity of the bombing, but also because the British aircraft were dropping newly developed incendiary bombs that were made of phosphorus. These created such an intense heat that – in the words of one eyewitness – "burning asphalt made the streets look like rivers of fire."

Every available fire engine was summoned to help, and by 0410 hours the city had been officially declared a major disaster area. Although strategic targets were hit, the bombing was indiscriminate and when the fires took hold they rampaged through everything in their path, including thousands of private houses.

At daybreak on July 25, a large greyish cloud hung like a pall over the city of Hamburg. Then, at 1634 hours, more than 200 daylight bombers of the USAAF arrived to carry on where the RAF had left off. After that assault, the night was quiet, but on the following day – July 26 – the American Flying Fortresses returned and strafed the stricken city yet again. Even then, the ordeal of the citizens of Hamburg was not over. On the night of July 27, 787 RAF bombers approached the city from the northeast. Nine districts east of the Alster were badly hit, the worst affected again being Borgfelde and Hamm.

By 0200 on the morning of the 28th, the last bombers turned back to base. Behind them, four square miles (6 sq km) of Hamburg were alight and 16,000 buildings were on fire. The firestorm that started on the night of July 27 raged until 0900 hours the following morning. The death toll of the raids and fires was put at 45,000.

Above: A building still burns as people pick their way through the rubble that was Hamburg.

Right: Some districts of the city were almost entirely flattened by the raids.

DRESDEN, GERMANY

FEBRUARY 13-17, 1945

Above: A year after the bombings and resulting firestorm, Dresden remained a wrecked city.

Before World War II, Dresden was known as "the flower of the Elbe" and was numbered among the world's most beautiful cities. The city's prewar population was about 600,000, but this rose during the war to about a million because it was widely believed the Allies would not bomb its historic buildings. During the latter part of the war, however, the city was almost completely destroyed in massive bombing raids carried out by the British RAF and the US Air Force. Much of the damage was caused when repeated bombing created a firestorm that swept through the city.

On February 13 at 2215 hours, 245 RAF Lancaster bombers flew over Dresden and dropped incendiaries and 2-ton bombs across the greater part of the city. The attack went on in waves. The incendiaries started thousands of small fires that rapidly came together in a single, great firestorm.

The intense heat of the resulting inferno created a huge column of smoke and flame that rose miles into the air and extended over a wide area. In the center of the vortex there was a terrific updraft of air. This created an area of low pressure at its base, and into the void rushed cooler surrounding air that fanned the flames even further. The winds thus generated were greater than those of a tornado. A tornado is thought to be caused by an increase in temperature of about 20 or 30 degrees Centigrade, but in the Dresden firestorm, the temperature is thought to have risen by as much as 1000 degrees Centigrade. This resulted in a fiery wind that rushed upwards at speeds of more than 100 mph (160 km/h).

At noon the following day, 450 B-17s of the United States Air Force came across and bombed central Dresden again. Then in the evening the RAF bombers returned – this time there were 550 of them.

German anti-aircraft in the area was inadequate and the Luftwaffe put up very little resistance in the air: only eight Allied bombers were shot down throughout the whole operation. It is impossible to be certain how many people died in these raids: estimates range between 60,000 and 135,000, most of whom were civilians. Total casualties are thought to have been in the region of 400,000.

Dresden continued to be bombarded by raids until April 17. Wave after wave of attacks obliterated the greater part of the city, which was so badly damaged that, at the end of the war later that year, it was suggested that it might be best to level the site and rebuild entirely.

Eventually, however, a compromise was reached: it was decided to rebuild the most important historic buildings, notably the Zwinger – a rococo-style museum on the southern bank of the River Elbe – and the baroque buildings around the castle, and create a new city in the area outside. Much of Dresden was reconstructed with modern, plain buildings, broad streets and squares, and green open spaces, with the aim of preserving as much of the city's former character as was possible in the circumstances.

Above: Dresden in 1946 – piles of rubble are testimony to the city's devastation.

Right: A photograph taken in April 1945 shows the ruins of the museum of fine arts.

TOKYO, JAPAN

MARCH 9-10, 1945

Right: Tokyo under attack. On the night of March 9, 1945, 280 USAF bombers subjected the capital of Japan to a raid of unprecedented ferocity.

At least 80,000 and possibly as many as 200,000 citizens of Tokyo were killed in a raid of low-level firebombing carried out by the United States Air Force (USAF) on the night of March 9–10, 1945. Although the exact number of dead will never be known, it is now thought that this raid claimed more victims than the atomic bomb that was dropped later that year on Hiroshima.

The attack began under cover of darkness at 2200 hours on the night of March 9. It was carried out by 280 USAF B-29 bombers which had been specially converted for the operation: all their armaments except their tail guns had been removed to accommodate the maximum weight of incendiary devices.

The first wave came in at an altitude of 5000 feet (1500m) and dropped napalm markers in the shape of a cross over the southeast of the Japanese capital. Subsequent streams of aircraft returned to describe a flaming circle around the four points of the cross. After

that, the object was to set fire to all four dark quadrants – an area of 15 square miles (40 sq km).

The night was clear and there was a strong breeze gusting to 40mph (65km/h). The wind fed the fire and the fire fed the wind until the blaze intensified into a great firestorm. Flames shot up in great dragon's tails so high into the air that the undersides of the bombers' fuselages were scorched black with soot.

Tokyo was devastated. The Japanese authorities had never prepared the city or its inhabitants to withstand a sustained aerial bombardment. Non-essential buildings had not been demolished to create firebreaks nor had women and children been evacuated to the countryside, precautions that had been taken in most strategically important cities throughout Europe. The terrified citizens of Tokyo ran out into the open spaces and took refuge on islands and in water. But the fire had become so intense that it jumped the urban canals and the Sumida River, setting fire to everyone and everything in its path.

Right: The industrial area of Tokyo along the Sumida River after the attack. Only modern buildings of steel or concrete survived the concentrated low-level firebombing.

Below: American soldiers inspect the wreckage of Tokyo after the end of World War II. The people of Tokyo were quite unprepared for an air raid or the firestorm that followed.

At the height of the attack and for several hours afterwards, the glow from the inferno was visible 150 miles (240km) away. At its heart, those who were not burned to death were suffocated for lack of oxygen and had their lungs seared by poisonous fumes. The experience of Fusako Sasaki was typical of thousands: "As I ran, I kept my eyes on the sky. It was like a fireworks' display as the incendiaries exploded. People were aflame, rolling and writhing in agony, screaming piteously for help but beyond all mortal assistance."

In addition to the dead, 1.8 million people were injured or made homeless. Tokyo's hospitals were ill-equipped to deal with a disaster of this magnitude: they had no plasma, no painkillers, not even bandages. The all-clear was finally sounded at 0500 hours on the morning of March 10, but it took four days to put out the fire and 25 days to clear up all the bodies.

The Tokyo massacre had been designed to bring Japan to its knees and force it to surrender. But in the short term it had the opposite effect. The people of Japan – of all classes – became determined that they must fight on because they were now convinced that the Americans were bent on the destruction of the entire Japanese nation.

ABADAN, IRAN

AUGUST 19, 1978

Of all the violent incidents in Iran during the year that preceded the Islamic Revolution and the overthrow of the Shah in January 1979, none aroused greater outrage than the firebombing of the Rex Cinema in the southern oil city of Abadan. A total of 377 people in the audience were killed when terrorists soaked the floors and walls of the cinema entrance with petrol and then set fire to them during a late night film.

The fire was started by Shi'ite extremists and was the worst in a long series of attacks on Western-style businesses such as banks, liquor stores, and restaurants, which were regarded by revolutionaries as a pernicious influence on the native culture. Indeed, this was the seventh time in a week that an Iranian cinema had been firebombed – in one of the earlier incidents,

in the holy city of Mashad, east of the capital Tehran, three members of the audience had been killed. The wave of atrocities took place during the holy month of Ramadan, when Muslims are supposed to fast and pray. The purpose of the outrages was to raise political tensions in the run-up to the anniversary of the assassination of Imam Ali, who is second only to the Prophet Muhammad as an object of veneration in Iran.

After the fire, the caretaker of the Rex was arrested for negligence. The police maintained that he was drunk on duty, but the real reason for the high death toll was that the doors were all locked shortly after the film began, probably in order to prevent latecomers getting in without paying.

In the circumstances, it is amazing that anyone came out alive, but 100 cinemagoers somehow managed to break their way out and escape from the

***Below:** The outside of the Rex cinema in Abadan after the firebombing.*

inferno uninjured. Witnesses later testified that the arsonists had taken time and trouble over their work and had left the petrol to seep in to the carpet before setting it ablaze. Members of the audience said that they had heard loud explosions just before flames shot up the cinema walls. At this point there was an immediate panic, and many people were trampled to death underfoot in the rush to escape. Others were burned to death or asphyxiated by toxic smoke fumes which belched out of the seats and other plastic furnishings. Nearly all the bodies were found in heaps behind doors which had not given way despite the frenzied battering they had taken.

Police later said that most of the victims were so badly burned that it was impossible to identify them, and they were all buried without due ceremony in a communal grave outside the city. This form of burial was against strict Islamic laws, and the police station was later besieged by 2000 angry and distraught bereaved relatives demanding decent treatment for the bodies of their loved ones.

RODO'S AND EL HUECO'S CLUBS, LONDON, ENGLAND

AUGUST 16, 1980

Thirty-seven people were burned to death or asphyxiated when two clubs in a single building in central London were firebombed by an arsonist with a grudge.

These establishments were not trendy night spots but illegal after-hours drinking clubs in Denmark Place, a sordid alleyway on the edge of Soho. Almost every-

thing about them was sleazy and even their names were unreliable – they were also known variously as the Colombian Club, the Spanish Club, and Victor's.

The man responsible for the deaths was John "Gypsy" Thompson. He torched the clubs because he thought he had been overcharged for a drink. Angry at having had to pay £5 ($8) for a rum and coke, he took a minicab to a nearby garage and bought a gallon (4.5 liters) of gasoline. At 0300 hours he went back to the building, poured the gasoline through the letter box, and threw a lighted match after it.

The flammable vapor caught light at once. There was a large explosion and a fireball rushed up the narrow staircase to the clubs on the two upper floors of the three-storey building. (The ground floor was used to store the barrows of traders who operated in the street during the day.) Within seconds the whole interior was engulfed in flames. People sitting at the bar on the first floor had no time to react and fell dead still clutching their drinks. On the top floor, some of the customers in El Hueco's had a moment's warning of the danger and rushed into the tiny kitchen at the rear, from which they tried to escape through a small window 2-feet (0.6m) square. A few managed to get out and slide to safety down the sloping roof below, but most were overwhelmed by the flames. The shambles in the kitchen showed that people had tried to climb over each other in a desperate fight to escape. As a police fire investigator put it: "There wouldn't have been room for them all to have stood normally in that small space."

The fire brigade brought the blaze under control at 0330 hours, but by then the building was gutted and part of the slate roof had collapsed. They found 24 victims in Rodo's and 13 in El Hueco's on the top floor. Most of the bodies were so badly mutilated that it was difficult to tell even what sex they were. This, together with the fact that most of the drinkers were illegal immigrants, made identification immensely difficult. Everyone was eventually named partly because some of the victims' passports contained their owners' fingerprints.

Although Thompson thought no one had seen him firebomb the clubs, he was identified by eyewitnesses. He was afterwards convicted of murder and sent to prison for life.

Left: *Firemen at work near the door (on the right) to the two clubs, which were on the upper floors of the building.*

SALANG PASS TUNNEL, AFGHAN

NOVEMBER 2 OR 3, 1982

At least 1000 and possibly as many as 2700 troops and civilians were burned to death or suffocated after fire broke out in a road tunnel through the mountainous Hindu Kush. The tragedy occurred during the USSR's long – and ultimately unsuccessful – military campaign (1979–1989) to take over Afghanistan.

The Salang Pass tunnel was the principal road link between Kabul, the Afghan capital, and the USSR. It was thus of great strategic importance to both sides in the conflict. The Soviet forces guarded it ferociously in order to keep their supply lines open and it was often the target of attacks by guerrillas of the Afghan Muslim resistance movement.

The Soviet-built tunnel was 1.7 miles (2.5km) long, 17 feet (5m) wide and 25 feet (7.5m) high; it was poorly ventilated and lay at an altitude of 11,000 feet (3300m).

The disaster began when a petrol tanker was involved in a head-on collision with the leading vehicle in a Soviet military convoy. The tanker burst into flames almost immediately and was destroyed along with about 30 other vehicles, including transport trucks and buses. Several hundred men were burned to death at once. Most of the victims, however, died from asphyxiation by inhaling exhaust fumes – this was because in winter, high in the mountains, it was intensely cold and vehicles further down the convoy – whose drivers may not even have realized what was happening – kept their engines running. This quickly created an unbearable build-up of poisonous gases in the confined area of the tunnel.

But the most important contributory factor to the enormous number of fatalities was that, on hearing the explosion, Soviet troops mistook it for an enemy attack and immediately closed the tunnel at both ends,

Below: A Soviet patrol guarding a mountain pass in Afghanistan. When the officer guarding the Salang Pass tunnel heard the explosion, he sealed off both ends of the tunnel, trapping everyone inside.

Above: The Hindu Kush mountain range, separating the USSR and Afghanistan, was traversed through the Salang Pass road tunnel.

trapping everyone inside. This meant that everyone inside the tunnel died. Four days after the accident, the bodies of Soviet victims were still being airlifted to Kabul, while the Afghan dead and injured were taken to Jellalabad near the Pakistan border.

One eyewitnesss said that shortly after the tragedy a Soviet investigator who had been sent to the scene had a violent public argument with the officer whose decision it had been to close the tunnel.

Other details of the tragedy are sketchy, because the movement of troops is always a closely guarded secret and in the former Soviet Union there was no uncensored news coverage in peacetime, let alone in time of war. Even the exact date of the Afghan tunnel disaster is unknown, although news of it had reached Western intelligence sources by November 9. It is thought that the disaster may have taken place during the late afternoon about one week previously.

THE MOVE FIRE, PHILADELPHIA, USA

MAY 15, 1985

At least 11 people – four of them children – were killed and more than 250 left homeless as fire swept through a row of 61 houses in Philadelphia, Pennsylvania, USA. The disaster occurred when police dropped a bomb on the headquarters of Move, a radical group which described itself as "anti-society" and claimed to have renounced modern technology and everything to do with the US establishment. But one thing was never clear: was the tragedy an accident or had the police taken a deliberate decision to use extreme force, no matter what the consequences might be to nearby property and human life?

The bombing ended a 24-hour siege at a house in Osage Avenue during which police had fought the armed radicals in an attempt to evict them from the building. "We did not create any fire," said Police Commissioner Sambor. "To the best of our knowledge, the Move members had spread flammable material in their compound and in the neighboring area."

Sambor's claim that the police had not known the danger until it was too late was backed by Wilson Goode, the Mayor of Philadelphia, who insisted that the fire had been an accident: he said that the bomb had been meant to knock out Move's rooftop fortifications and open the way for the use of tear gas or water

Above: Clouds of black smoke rise over a residential street in Philadelphia after the police bombed a house belonging to Move, a radical, anti-social group.

43

Right: The fire spread rapidly through a row of 61 houses, leaving more than 250 people homeless, and 11 people dead.

Below: An armed policeman keeps watch on the fire created by the bombing.

to clear out the group without the danger of any loss of life. Explosives would not have been used, he said, if the authorities had known that there was flammable material in the house.

Asked why the fire brigade had not begun to tackle the blaze until it had been raging for at least an hour, city officials explained that the firemen were afraid they might be shot at – but the fire commissioner had already gone on record saying that leaving the fire to burn "worked to the city's advantage."

Many important questions remained unanswered: why had the bomb been dropped after Move had apparently announced over the loudspeaker system – with which they regularly harangued local residents – that they had gasoline in the house? Why had the police attacked when they knew that there were children inside the building? One member of the group – a woman known as Ramona Africa (all Move members took the surname Africa) – was arrested after escaping from the burned-out house and charged with making terrorist threats. In court, she asked the judge: "When are you going to charge Wilson Goode with murder?"

As the fire raged uncontrolled, many other houses in the street were destroyed and 250 people unconnected with Move were left homeless. Despite being promised that all the buildings would be rebuilt by Christmas, the residents sued the City of Philadelphia, its mayor and police chief for 10 million dollars. Later that year, under intense media scrutiny, Police Commissioner Sambor resigned from his post.

KUWAIT OIL FIELDS

FEBRUARY-NOVEMBER 1991

Above:
Firefighters direct hoses on a burning oil well from behind a fire shield.

Right: The heat generated by the fires was so intense that it was impossible for the firefighters to get near without the help of heat shields.

Early in 1991, at the end of the Gulf War, the armed forces of Iraq were forcibly driven out of Kuwait – which they had invaded during the previous year – by the combined strength of the United States and their allies. As the Iraqi forces withdrew, they loosed a telling parting shot which caused enormous damage to Kuwait's ecology and economy. On February 22, 1991, Iraqi engineers detonated thousands of pounds (kilograms) of explosives which had been laid against 810 of occupied Kuwait's 940 active oil wells. Of these, 730 exploded. Those that did not catch fire gushed crude oil uncontrollably from their shattered well heads. A total of 656 oil wells were left burning — giving a new meaning to the term "scorched earth policy".

The resulting inferno burned for nine months. The greater part of the whole country was left ablaze, and this led to the loss of up to 1.5 billion barrels of oil, worth some $27 billion. The oil flared off into the sky or became dumped in thick, tar-like lakes at the rate of about 6 million barrels a day. Conservative estimates put the total loss at about 67 million tonnes of oil. In addition, the resulting smoke plumes – which were so thick and rose so high into the air that they were clearly visible from space – produced an estimated 2.1 million tonnes of soot particles and more than 2 million tonnes of sulphur.

The knock-on effects were wide reaching. As far away as the Himalayas, snow became blackened with particles of soot and coal tar which had been blown right across Asia from the seat of the inferno; sheep grazing over a thousand miles (16,000km) away had their fleeces covered with a thick brown wind-borne residue. A slick of oil, immeasurably greater than that emitted from the Exxon Valdez in Alaska in 1989, drifted 350 miles (560km) down the Gulf coastline before it was halted at Abu Ali island. Meanwhile, in Kuwait City itself, day would be turned into night in a moment, depending on the direction of the wind. Many Kuwaitis and Iraqis were injured by inhaling lung-damaging sulphurous fumes.

And yet, the blaze which ranks in intensity with the worse incendiary bombing raids on Dresden and Tokyo during World War II, was eventually brought under control much more quickly and painlessly than analysts had predicted. Better still, not a single fatality was added to the roll of war dead.

The first fire, in the Ahmadi Oil Field, was put out on March 18 by US Army Sergeant Forrest Irvin, who

Below: The cumbersome firefighting equipment necessary to deal with the fires was in short supply. Initially the single road from the Saudi border to Kuwait City was blocked with slow-moving, heavy civilian and military traffic. The only other way to get the equipment in was to fly it in to Kuwait international airport.

Above: A giant chimney is maneuvered over the head of a burning oil well. When the chimney was firmly bedded down over the well head, the flames coming out of the top of the chimney would be extinguished using sea water or a fire-quenching gas. The well head would then be capped.

Right: The burning oil wells belched plumes of dark, acrid smoke into the atmosphere, turning the sky dark.

tossed a grenade into the neck of the blaze and cut off the flame: the success of this technique led to it being widely used to put out the other blazes.

Firefighters from many parts of the world were rushed to Kuwait, including the US firefighting team led by the charismatic but aging Red Adair. The work of the firefighters was dirty and dangerous. Sometimes the explosives had not gone off, and had to be removed – a job that should have been done by bomb removal experts. Since there were none available the firefighters had to do it themselves. The burning wells had to be capped. Even getting near them was difficult since the heat from the blaze was terrific. Sometimes more explosives were used to extinguish the blaze.

Operation Desert Quench, as it was called, employed 1200 men, working from dawn to dusk in the desert heat. "Some wells will take three or four months to put out, and the worst are yet to come," said Red Adair in the first weeks. By July it was estimated that 80 percent of the world's oil firefighting capability was gathered in Kuwait, but even so the firefighting efforts were hampered by lack of equipment.

It was November before the last of the screaming banshee blazes was finally quelled. "It's great to hear the silence after you stop a real ripper," said Maurice Engman, a field hand with one of the firefighting companies. On November 6, the last burning well head was ceremonially extinguished by the Emir of Kuwait. But the economic damage was lasting. As a direct result of Iraq's tactics, the cost of Kuwaiti oil rose from 80 cents to between $3 and $4 per barrel.

Left: After each fire was put out, the firefighters had to cap the well to stop the crude oil gushing out. Up to 1.5 billion barrels of oil was lost – much of it being dumped on the ground – worth about $27 billion.

LA FENICE THEATER, VENICE, ITALY

JANUARY 29, 1996

Left: Venice's world famous opera house, La Fenice, was still smoldering the day after the blaze that substantially destroyed it. La Fenice ("The Phoenix") was no stranger to fire. The original theater had been built in the late 18th century on the site of an earlier building razed by fire, and in 1836, only 38 years after its opening, the theater was burned to the ground. It was rebuilt (hence its name, "The Phoenix") and staged the opening nights of many famous grand operas.

The Teatro la Fenice is one of the world's oldest and most famous grand opera venues. Built in the rococo style during the 18th century, it has staged the first performances of works by Verdi, Rossini, Wagner, and Stravinsky. When much of the interior was reduced to ashes late one winter's night, it was as clear a case of arson as could be imagined. Not long afterwards, the Italian authorities took the unusual step of announcing publicly that they knew how and why it happened and even, in general terms, the people responsible. Despite that, no one has ever been arrested or charged with the crime.

The fire bore the classic signs of a deliberate attack. The person or persons unknown who started it knew exactly what they were doing – they were intimately familiar with the layout of the building and laid their fire near the roof where it would cause the maximum damage in the shortest time. They struck when people with inside information would have known that the place would be unoccupied and even that the night-watchman would not be on duty. Neither, probably, was it a coincidence that the fire broke out shortly after the nearby canals had been drained for cleaning and therefore the fire barges were unable to get close enough to tackle the blaze.

The alarm was raised late at night when passers-by saw flames and smoke rising from the roof of La Fenice. Firefighting was difficult since the theater was beyond the reach of canal-borne emergency services and there are no roads in Venice. One brave helicopter pilot bombarded the fire with water which he scooped out of the Venice Lagoon.

The most widely accepted and publicly aired theory was that the fire was started deliberately to avoid a contractual dispute between the owners and the builders who had been carrying out extensive refurbishment works to the interior of the theater. The contractors had fallen badly behind schedule and the destruction of a large part of La Fenice meant that the theater owners would not be able to invoke a penalty clause which, after a certain date, would have cost the builders £20,000 ($32,000) every day.

All the evidence subsequently gathered by Felice Casson, the Chief Magistrate of Venice, pointed to arson. A year later, everyone seemed to agree that it had been the work of the Mafia. But the investigation did not name names and a year later the Italian police were no nearer to making an arrest. Massimo Cacciari, the left-wing Mayor of Venice, supported Signor Casson and his findings, but complained: "Saying La Fenice was burned down by Cosa Nostra [the Mafia] is about as useful as saying that it was attacked by alien spacecraft."

Following the fire it was estimated that the new refurbishment works to La Fenice would now cost around £49 million ($80 million).

Left: *The scene of devastation inside the historic opera house after the fire.*

Right: *Fighting the blaze was made difficult by the fact that the nearby canals had been drained and it was impossible to get fire barges close to the theater.*

PUBLIC PLACES

Some of the most catastrophic fire disasters have occurred in public places – bars, cinemas, football stands, hotels, night clubs, theaters. Although these are all buildings dedicated to leisure activities, it would be wrong to conclude from this that human beings are never in greater danger than when they are relaxed. Such places are generally safe – even when a fire breaks out, they may not be death traps as long as there are sufficient fire extinguishers and enough exits through which to make an orderly evacuation.

But in the most horrific cases that follow, the victims have found themselves trapped inside burning buildings with no way out and no equipment with which to fight the fire. Sometimes, they panicked and failed to behave logically – this may explain what happened in the church at Costesti in Romania. But elsewhere, people died unnecessarily for sordid reasons – the audience in the Statuto Cinema, Turin, Italy, was immured in a furnace because the management had locked the exits to prevent latecomers getting in without paying. It is no matter whether one blames the officials or those who tried to avoid buying tickets – tragedies like these are the most terrifying of all.

Some of the fires in this chapter made headlines because many people died in them. Others were newsworthy because there was particular interest in the buildings themselves and their contents. Many people mourned the destruction of the Crystal Palace as they would the loss of a friend; the restoration of English royal treasures remained a topic of great public interest for five years after they were damaged in a fire at Windsor Castle.

Right: When fire broke out in a top floor "grace and favor" apartment in England's historic Hampton Court Palace, it caused the death of an elderly resident and damage worth over £1 million ($2.63 million).

IROQUOIS THEATER, CHICAGO, USA

DECEMBER 30, 1903

A total of 578 people were killed by a fire which swept through the Iroquois Theater, Chicago, USA, in December 1903. A huge matinee audience was watching a Christmas show when the auditorium was suddenly engulfed in flames from a fire that had started backstage. One of the most bitter ironies of this disaster was that Chicago had already been razed to the ground once in October 1871, and many of the new public buildings which had risen, phoenix-like, from the ashes had been designed and constructed with fire safety as the highest priority.

The Iroquois had been completed only the previous month. Posters advertising the inaugural Christmas production of *Mr Bluebeard*, a popular entertainment of the period, described the theater as "absolutely fireproof". *Mr Bluebeard* had attracted standing-room only houses throughout the Christmas period, and on the afternoon of the tragedy there was an audience of about 2000 in a theater with seats for only 1600.

When the fire broke out, comedian Eddie Foy, who was on stage at the time, appealed for an orderly exit, but to little avail. The performers and stagehands escaped immediately through the stage door, but there

Left: The shambles inside the theater after the fire. The theater had been completed only a month earlier, and its opening production was billed as a "great spectacular entertainment from the Theater Royal, Drury Lane, London". The theater was completely full at the time of the fire.

Above: The auditorium of the theater was opulently decorated and furnished, and the upholstery on the seating burned fiercely, belching out smoke and fumes that suffocated many of the trapped audience.

were not enough exits from the auditorium to cope with the mass of people. The exits from the stalls led into narrow alleyways, while those from the balcony and circle all joined up into a single passageway, thus funneling people into a crowd that could not disperse in time to avert disaster.

Inevitably, a great crush ensued and the doors soon became jammed with terrified people who panicked in the scramble for safety. Some jumped from the balcony into the pit; others jumped from external fire escapes to their death in the street below. Those who did not reach the exits at all were either burned to death or suffocated by fumes and dense smoke belching out from the upholstery. About 200 people died in this way, but almost twice as many were trampled to death in the stampede to get out – many bodies had boot marks all over their faces.

Fire does its work quickly, and the Iroquois was completely gutted in less than ten minutes. Reputedly the safest public building in Chicago, the theater in fact violated numerous safety laws, including strict rules about overcrowding, and five employees were subsequently charged with manslaughter. Although there was a safety curtain – an essential anti-fire feature in any theater – in the emergency it did not perform its intended function of cutting off the auditorium from the stage area where there are always numerous flammable materials such as greasepaint and wooden scenery. On the afternoon of the fire, the safety curtain seems to have jammed briefly and then been lowered, but only after flames had crossed the threshold between stage and auditorium.

In the aftermath of the blaze, 50 theaters elsewhere in the USA were closed for safety reasons.

COSTESTI CHURCH, ROMANIA

APRIL 18, 1930

Costesti is a small and remote town in the foothills of the Carpathians about 60 miles (96km) northwest of the Romanian capital, Bucharest. On the evening of Good Friday in 1930 the Orthodox church there was destroyed by a fire in which 140 worshippers died and many more were seriously injured.

The little parish church, a wooden structure more than 100 years old, was packed for the evening service. A lighted candle held by one of the congregation accidentally set fire to a decorative wreath – in a moment the whole building was filled with flames and smoke.

The congregation immediately panicked and rushed straight for the door. But tragically the heavy wooden door opened inwards and the force of the crowd crushing against it kept it tightly closed. Everyone was trapped inside. A few people standing outside in a passageway tried to push their way in, but they were unable to do anything because of the enormous weight of people behind the door.

The alarm was raised immediately but the church was some distance from the town and by the time help arrived it was too late. Someone telephoned the nearest fire station at Pitesti, but this was 15 miles (24 km) to the north and the fire engines drove up just as the roof collapsed. The 140 men, women, and children still inside the church were buried under a heavy mass of burning wood. Two hours later, the fire was extinguished – but all that remained of the church was a smoldering ruin.

Above: A typical traditional Romanian village church, built of wood. It was in such a church at Costesti that 140 people perished.

Right: The door of the church was a heavy timber door that opened inwards. The crush of panic-stricken people attempting to get out of the burning building prevented the door from opening.

CRYSTAL PALACE, LONDON, ENGLAND

NOVEMBER 30, 1936

Crystal Palace – a huge glass conservatory built to house the Great Exhibition of 1851 – was originally sited in Hyde Park. After the exhibition it was moved to the top of a ridge 300 feet (90m) high at Sydenham in southeast London, where it was turned into a concert hall and the focal point of a great amusement park. Here it remained until the last night of November, 1930, when it was razed to the ground in a fire so spectacular that it was clearly visible from as far away as the coastal towns of Brighton and Margate.

Flames were first noticed in the central part of the great structure at about 1930 hours. A musician who had just arrived to take part in a choir practice saw the fire but was told not to worry, it would soon be out, and to carry on with his rehearsal. Three hours later, however, more than two-thirds of the Crystal Palace were lying on the ground in a flaring mass of ruins. Even then the fire raged on unchecked, fanned by a strong northwesterly breeze.

The roof – 400 tons of glass – had been the first part of the structure to succumb and crash to the ground. Then the huge skeleton of the building – 4000 tons of iron girders – bent and twisted before falling in an immense shower of sparks. The Palace's 200 miles (300 km) of wooden window frames burnt like match sticks and helped to spread the conflagration.

When the alarm was raised the permanent fire-fighting force attached to the Palace did their utmost with the limited resources at their disposal, but it quickly became apparent that their efforts were hopeless. By the time the first outside aid arrived from the fire station at nearby Penge, the whole of the central transept was ablaze. Before long, firemen from all over London arrived to help – their 20 hoses needed so much water that domestic supplies were reduced to half pressure throughout the night. Even this was insufficient, and the emergency reservoir and tanks had to be brought into use.

Flames rose more than 150 feet (45m) above the Palace. The pilot of an Imperial Airways aircraft reported that he could see the fire from the middle of the English Channel. Thousands of people throughout

Left: The Crystal Palace was built by Joseph Paxton to house the Great Exhibition of 1851 in Hyde Park. The building was later dismantled and moved to Sydenham.

London and southeast England noticed the great glare in the distance and set out to get a closer view of the inferno – the destruction of this great building became a tourist attraction, later described as "the best show in town". Special trains were run to bring sightseers from central London and there were mile-long traffic jams on all roads leading to the fire. Yet, although there is no doubt that these crowds hampered efforts to contain the fire, their interest was not altogether ghoulish – throughout the throng there were expressions of sadness at the end of "the poor old Palace".

Despite the size of the blaze, no one was seriously injured. The main casualties were thousands of birds which were released from an aviary in the grounds for their own safety but were then overcome by smoke and crashed to their deaths in the flames.

Above: After the fire little remained of the great glass and iron Palace but a mass of twisted girders.

Left: The death of an historic building. The heat of the fire melted the iron structure and brought the glass crashing to the ground.

COCOANUT GROVE CLUB, BOSTON, USA

NOVEMBER 28, 1942

At the height of World War II, the USA was rocked by a domestic tragedy unconnected with the hostilities. A sudden fire ripped through Cocoanut Grove Night Club in Boston, Massachusetts, at about 2200 hours on the night of November 28. More than 300 people were killed – some estimates put the figure as high as 474 – and a further 150 were seriously injured.

After extensive interior refurbishment during the previous year, Cocoanut Grove had become one of the most fashionable spots in the Boston midtown district. On the night of the tragedy, it was full to bursting with US sailors, marines, and coastguardsmen – many on leave from active service in Europe – with their wives and girlfriends. There were also many American football fans who earlier that day had been to a game in which under-dogs Holy Cross had beaten red-hot favorites Boston by 55 to 12. The exact number in the club at the time is unknown, but it is thought to have been in the region of 1000.

The new decor featured simulated leather chairs, plastic palm trees, and a silk-draped roof. The style was one of the club's chief draws – but it also made it a deathtrap. At 2217 hours, the performers had just gone out on stage: bandleader Micky Alpert started

Right: *The scene outside the Cocoanut Grove club as the dead are carried out in the aftermath of the horrific fire that killed over 300 people.*

Above: Firemen inspect the revolving doors at the rear of the Cocoanut Grove. These led to a tiny vestibule where panicking guests were crushed and smothered as they fought to get out of the burning building.

one of the plastic palm trees, which went up in a moment. The fire spread rapidly and poisonous fumes belched out of the molten plastic walls.

The clubbers panicked and rushed for the doors, but the exits were not signposted and at least one of the escape routes was locked. Those who found their way back to the entrance in the Melody Lounge became wedged in and around the revolving door – many of the victims were found in this area, either crushed or overcome by smoke.

The gallant efforts of Marshall Cook, a south Boston boy dancer, saved at least 35 – mainly artistes – as he led them to safety up a ladder and across the roof to adjacent buildings. Although the fire brigade arrived quickly, they could not get into the club because of the pile of bodies already obstructing the entrance. On arrival at Boston City Hospital, many of the dead were found to be so badly burned that it proved impossible to identify them.

The official inquiry into Cocoanut Grove, published in November 1943, found that the club had been a disaster looking for an opportunity to happen. The decorations were unsafe, the sprinkler system was inadequate, and the exits not properly signposted. The Boston City Building Commissioner and a senior policeman were indicted but subsequently acquitted. However, one of the club's owners was jailed for 12 years for failing to make adequate safety provisions.

playing "The Star-Spangled Banner" to announce the beginning of the entertainment. At the same time, a young waiter named Stephen Tomaszewski went to change a broken light bulb on one of the tables.

The club was dimly lit, so he struck a match to help him see what he was doing and accidentally set fire to

Right: A view of the interior of the club after the fire. The plastic palm trees and silk hangings of the club's decor had ignited quickly, making the place a deathtrap.

WINECOFF HOTEL, ATLANTA, USA

DECEMBER 7, 1946

A total of 137 people were killed on the night of December 7, 1946, when fire engulfed the 15-storey Winecoff Hotel in the heart of the business district of Atlanta, Georgia, USA. As many as 116 were pronounced dead at the scene; another 21 people died later in hospital from agonizing burns or the effects of smoke inhalation.

When any tall building catches fire, people on the upper floors are faced with a terrible choice. They can either jump immediately, risking almost certain death, or wait inside the building in the hope that help will reach them before they are engulfed in flames or overcome by smoke.

In the Winecoff tragedy, the death toll was highest among those who stayed in their rooms – almost 100 perished in this way, including the owner of the hotel, 70-year-old W.F. Winecoff, who had built the hotel in 1913 and had latterly been a resident.

But many of those who left by the windows also died, including 25 people who jumped from the upper storeys and were killed by the impact on landing. Some others tried to climb down ropes made out of bedsheets which had been hastily tied together – too hastily, as it turned out. The sheets were not knotted securely enough to take the weight and these people too fell to their deaths.

Most of those who survived were rescued by firemen – some climbed down ladders which had been cranked up to the high windows, while others leaped from as high as the tenth floor into outstretched jump-nets made of rope.

Left: Firemen direct streams of water through high-powered hoses into the upper floors of the Winecoff Hotel, situated in Atlanta's famous Peachtree Street. Many of the occupants of the 350 rooms in the hotel were asleep when fire swept through the building in the early hours of a Saturday morning. Of those who died in the fire, a number were killed when they jumped to their deaths from the upper storeys of the hotel.

LOEBEL CAFE, BERLIN, GERMANY

FEBRUARY 8, 1947

A fire at the Loebel Café – a dance hall at Hakenfelde in Spandau in the British-occupied sector of postwar Berlin – killed 80 of about 1000 people who had been enjoying a fancy-dress party and stage show.

The fire broke out at about 2230 hours and was probably caused by a faulty electric fuse or a defective chimney. Just after the cabaret had finished, sparks were seen passing along the ceiling.

At first, some of the guests thought this was part of the entertainment, some kind of special effect, but then a wooden beam caught light and the hall – a rambling, wooden building – was quickly engulfed in flames. Survivors later described how the atmosphere in the Café had remained calm until someone broke a window. At almost exactly that moment, a sheet of flame spread across the room; then there was panic, and a stampede for the main exit.

But the lobby was already blocked with people who had gone to collect their coats. In only a matter of minutes, the living throng here had been turned into a pile of dead bodies. Although some people made their escape through the two side entrances, many were trapped upstairs where the windows were barred.

The German fire brigade was assisted by the British fire brigade from Spandau, but their efforts were hampered by bad weather. It was one of the coldest nights of the year and much of the water was frozen. For a crucial period only one hose was operating.

Right: A crowded nightclub in postwar Berlin. It was in a similar venue – the Loebel Café – that fire broke out on the night of February 8, 1947, killing 80 people.

OUR LADY OF THE ANGELS SCHOOL, CHICAGO, USA

DECEMBER 1, 1958

Ninety-three people, most of them children, were killed when fire raced through a school in Chicago, USA, on the afternoon of December 1. The blaze was caused by an explosion in the boiler room: fanned by an icy wind the flames swept rapidly through the brick building.

The fire broke out at Our Lady of the Angels school on the city's West Side only 18 minutes before classes were due to be dismissed for the afternoon. There were 1300 pupils and staff in the school at the time. Although most were led unhurt to safety, many children and several teachers were trapped at their desks where they burned to death or were overcome by smoke. The death toll was particularly high on the second floor – in one classroom there, rescuers later found the bodies of 22 children and two nuns. Another 100 or so people were taken to hospital: many of these were badly burned or suffering the effects of smoke inhalation, while others were injured after jumping from upstairs windows.

That there were not even more fatalities was due largely to the prompt action of staff and passers-by. As soon as screams were heard, priests and nuns dashed from the rectory next door with blankets and towels and tried to rescue those trapped inside the brick school building. Three men who happened to be walking past the school hurried in to help but, tragically, they were overcome by heat and were among those killed. The fire brigade was quickly at the scene, as were all available doctors and nurses who treated many victims on the spot.

Right: School was almost over for the day when fire raced through the Our Lady of the Angels building, filling the upper floors with toxic fumes. Many pupils were saved by climbing down firemen's ladders, but 87 children and three nuns died in the blaze.

Right: After Chicago's worst school fire, firemen inspect one of the gutted corridors in the building.

For those who were not engulfed in flames, the main danger was from toxic fumes. Thomas Raymond, a 12-year-old pupil, later described how smoke had filled his upstairs classroom and the only way he could get fresh air was by lying on the floor. Then he broke the window by throwing books at it – he was preparing to jump when the fire brigade warned him not to. Thomas was one of many who clambered to safety down the firemen's ladder.

One brave nun singlehandedly saved 30 or 40 children from the fumes by making them crawl along the floor of the upstairs corridor and then rolling them down the stairs. Other children threw themselves onto the floor where the air was less smoky and kept still: most of these survived, although, by the time help arrived, many had been overcome by fumes and were pulled out unconscious.

As the fire still raged, the Chicago Fire Commissioner told the press "this could have been a touch-off" – American fireman's slang for arson. But subsequent investigations revealed that the disaster had been entirely accidental. Eleven-year-old Joseph Brocato told a doctor that he and a classmate had been emptying a wastepaper basket in the basement when they heard "a boom in the furnace room". Then the janitor ran out and shouted to them to get upstairs.

Right: An aerial view of the fire. Smoke pours from the building as firemen battle with the blaze. A crowd of over 10,000 people, many of them hysterical parents, had to be restrained by a police cordon. Of the 100 children brought out alive and taken to hospital, many were badly injured.

L'INNOVATION, BRUSSELS, BELGIUM

MAY 22, 1967

Three hundred and twenty-two people were killed in a fire which almost completely destroyed L'Innovation, a large department store in the Rue Neuve in the downtown district of Brussels, Belgium.

The fire started in the furniture department on the fourth floor during the lunchtime rush hour. The shop would have been busy with shopping crowds at this time on any day, but today it was particularly full with visitors to the first day of "American Fortnight", a huge

Left: Despite the strenuous efforts of the firefighting forces the largest department store in Brussels, L'Innovation, was almost entirely destroyed by a fire that started on the fourth floor during the busy lunchtime shopping period.

Far right: When the smoke finally cleared from the ruins of the department store, only a heap of charred rubble remained.

in-store exhibition of US merchandise. There are thought to have been at least 1000 people on the premises at the time of the outbreak. To mark the occasion, much of the inside of the shop had been specially decorated with Stars and Stripes flags – these added fuel to the blaze, as too did a large stock of paper dresses specially imported from the US.

The alarm system did not go off – probably because the fire had knocked out the electrical systems – and thus many shoppers remained unaware of the danger they were in even after flames became readily visible from the outside of the building. Although an alternative signal was given, most customers failed to understand the significance of repeated ringing of the service bell.

The fire quickly gained a strong hold and violent explosions shook L'Innovation every few minutes. The blaze raged out of control and soon threatened to spread to a large number of adjacent buildings on the block. One whole side of the store collapsed with a roar, covering fire engines in rubble but miraculously injuring none of the firemen.

However, Deputy Fire Chief Jacques Mesmans broke both his legs after picking up a woman and jumping with her in his arms out of a second floor window. Many of those trapped high up the building

Below: As a pall of black smoke rose over the blazing building, many shoppers leaped to their deaths from upper floor windows, their clothes in flames.

faced the desperate choice between jumping and burning. Three people were killed by leaping from the roof, where they had been trapped by flames. Meanwhile, many others perished horribly as they were transformed into living torches on window ledges in full view of the world.

As the first people were led out through the main exit, one man rushed in and started looting the store. He was quickly overpowered and taken away by police.

After the fire, L'Innovation and two surrounding blocks had to be demolished: they had been due for redevelopment anyway. There was speculation at the time that the fire may have been started deliberately by anti-American demonstrators, but this was never proved – a likelier cause seems to have been an electrical fault or a carelessly discarded cigarette butt.

CLUB CINQ-SEPT, GRENOBLE, FRANCE

NOVEMBER 1, 1970

Left: The ruins of the Cinq-Sept club after the fire in which 146 young people died.

A blaze which began accidentally when a lighted match fell onto a plastic foam cushion ended shortly afterwards in the death of 146 young people. The tragedy took place at a night club in Saint-Laurent-du-Pont, a village in a forested area about 20 miles (32km) outside Grenoble, France.

The high death toll in this disaster was entirely due to the lack of normal safety precautions and safety equipment in a dance hall that was little more than a barn in the middle of nowhere.

Club Cinq-Sept was a popular disco which drew young people with cars from as far afield as Annecy, Chambéry, and Grenoble. It had an interior gallery which ran around its perimeter and overlooked the dance floor and stage. The whole place was decorated in the psychedelic manner of the period – there were revolving colored light displays and its alcoves were decked out to look like grottoes. But it had no licence for dancing, it was badly lit, badly ventilated, had no mains water and no windows.

As a small fire turned into an inferno – fed by an array of cheap plastic furnishings – dense acrid fumes quickly filled the whole venue. The audience – who had been listening to a set by an up-and-coming group from Paris called The Storm – panicked and struggled towards the exits, but when they reached them they found that they had been padlocked to keep out gatecrashers. They banged desperately on the doors but could not break them down and there was no one to unlock them – the two managers who were keyholders were among the fire's first victims.

Most of the 30 people who escaped did so by squeezing their way back out through the "in" turnstile. Twelve of these survivors were badly burned. Nearly

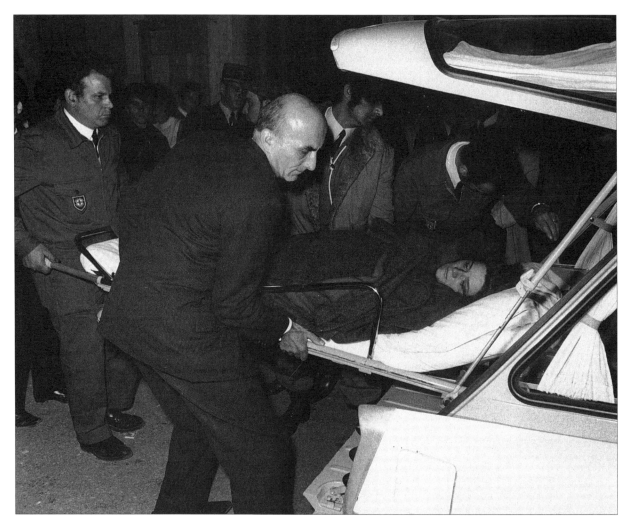

Right: A survivor from the dance-hall catastrophe is taken away to the hospital.

Below: Firemen searching the debris in the remains of the gutted Cinq-Sept club.

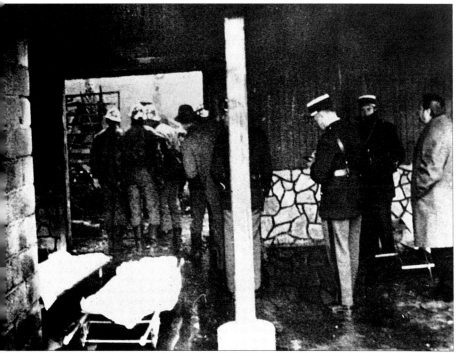

all the victims died through inhalation of toxic fumes and were asphyxiated before the flames reached them. Nevertheless, very few of the bodies were recognizable and most could be identified only by their jewelry, keys, and rings.

The one manager to survive the inferno was called Gilbert Bas. He afterwards described how he had been sitting in the club office when he had seen the alarm signal – a double flashing light – go off on his console. He at first assumed that it was the usual thing – another fist fight at the door – but when he got out onto the dance floor he heard cries of "fire!" He raced out of the club and drove straight to Saint-Laurent to raise the alarm. He felt there was nothing else he could do – Club Cinq-Sept did not even have a telephone.

Many fires gut the insides of a building but leave the exterior largely undamaged. The blaze at Club Cinq-Sept was different – by the time the emergency services arrived, even the corrugated iron roof had been melted by the heat of the flames. "The place went up like a matchbox," said one fireman sadly. "They didn't have a chance."

THE SENNICHI BUILDING, OSAKA, JAPAN

MAY 13, 1972

Below: A busy street in the centre of Osaka. The Sennichi department store in the city center caught fire late at night, killing 118 people and gutting the building.

A discarded cigarette or a small electrical fault was the most likely cause of a fire that gutted the seven-storey Sennichi department store building in Osaka, Japan, killing 118 people in a rooftop night club. A number of people died when they jumped off the parapet to escape the flames, but most of the victims were found in the nightclub, having succumbed to smoke and poisonous gases. Some died so quickly they had not even time to panic – one body was found with a hand outstretched as if about to pay for a drink.

The fire broke out late at night on the third floor of the building where construction work had been in progress for some time. It spread quickly through the darkened upper floors and then burst out onto the top level in the Play Town Club, a busy hostess bar with cabaret floor show.

There was no warning – the fire suddenly surged through the floor and walls and took its first victims before they realized what was happening. Then there was panic, and terrified hostesses and customers began to stampede through the smoke and flames toward the main door. Many of them died before they could reach the exit – they were either overcome by smoke or trampled to death in the crush. Others frantically smashed windows and leaped to their deaths. Eye-witnesses watched helplessly as people clung to the window ledges for a few moments before crashing onto the street below. One of the first people to arrive

67

Below: As flames and smoke swept through the Sennichi building, some people panicked and jumped to their deaths.

on the scene, a doctor, likened the carnage at the foot of the building to a plane crash.

Then the emergency services arrived in force, enabling 49 people to escape unhurt down fire brigade ladders. But the two tubular canvas chutes that were sent up from ground level to speed the evacuation proved disastrous – some people, too frightened of the smoke and flames to form a queue, tried to climb down the outside of the chutes but lost their grip and fell to their deaths; others who slid down the inside of the chute as they were meant to do shot out at the bottom, which was unattended, and were killed by the impact.

The following day, an electrician who had been working on the third floor was arrested on a charge of negligence. The inquiry into the Sennichi fire found that although the building did have a smokeproof emergency staircase from top to bottom it was unaccountably locked on the night of the tragedy.

SUMMERLAND LEISURE CENTER, ISLE OF MAN

AUGUST 2, 1973

Right: The Summerland indoor leisure center on the promenade at Douglas, Isle of Man, had been open barely a year before disaster struck.

Fifty people were killed when Summerland, a leisure center on the promenade at Douglas, Isle of Man, burned down in minutes after a small fire quickly became uncontrollable. It was the worst tragedy in Manx history.

Opened in 1972, Summerland was a state-of-the-art indoor tourist leisure center designed to provide "total entertainment" for families where parents could drink or dance on the top floor while their children played under supervision in other areas. It featured a wide range of attractions, including a basement funfair, discothèque, and solarium.

Summerland was an immediate hit with summer visitors and in its first year of operation managed to attract some 13 percent of the island's total tourist revenue. It was particularly crowded on the night of

August 2, partly because it was a new and popular attraction, and partly because the day outside had been cold and drizzly.

It is estimated that about 2000 people were enjoying themselves in the complex when, just before 2000 hours on Thursday evening, a small fire – thought to have been caused by an electrical fault – broke out near a yellow, artificially thatched amusement kiosk on the first floor terrace. Eye witnesses reported that within minutes the four-storey building was ablaze from end to end. The fire brigade was called and reached the scene within four minutes, but they were already too late.

The complex had an overall roof made of acrylic sheeting. This US product, known as Oroglas, had been marketed as "slow-burning plastic", but it turned out to melt and burn very quickly indeed. At the height of the

Right: Within minutes of the fire starting, black smoke was pouring out of the fun complex as people inside sought to escape. Several of the emergency exits were found to be blocked or jammed.

Above: Acrylic sheeting lining the roof of the complex caught fire and burned quickly. Within 20 minutes the inside of the building was gutted.

fire, a huge pall of black smoke rose several hundred feet into the air above Douglas Bay and flames shot higher than the cliff face into which Summerland had been grafted.

Liquid plastic rained down onto the tourists as they made a terrible stampede for the exits. One said: "I saw a man with his hair on fire and the coat melted off his back and a youngster in his arms." Several emergency doors were blocked or had become jammed: some people were able to break the glass and climb to safety, but many were not so fortunate.

The whole center quickly became a fireball. Although every available resource on the island was deployed – 15 fire appliances and more than 100 firemen – the building was gutted within 20 minutes. In an emergency medical airlift, plasma and blood were flown from Liverpool on the English mainland, 80 miles (128km) away.

The subsequent inquiry into the causes of the Summerland blaze blamed the choice of construction materials, many of which would not have been permitted on the mainland. The Isle of Man, though part of the British Isles, is not a part of the United Kingdom – it has its own separate government and laws.

THE JOELMA BUILDING, SAO PAULO, BRAZIL

FEBRUARY 1, 1974

When an office building in the center of São Paulo, Brazil, mysteriously caught fire on the morning of February 1, 1974, many of the workers inside were trapped on the upper floors of the building beyond the reach of the fire brigade's longest extending ladders. Though this might suggest a very tall skyscraper like those in New York, the Joelma Building was only 25 storeys high.

Left: *As flames and smoke engulf the Joelma Building, a man leaps from the roof to his death.*

Above: A helicopter lands on the roof to pick up survivors. The intense heat prevented helicopters from landing while the building was ablaze.

The bottom six floors of the Joelma Building were a multi-storey parking lot, above which were 19 floors of offices, including the headquarters of the Crefisul Bank. Altogether, 600 people were working in the building that day, and there were also about 100 visitors and customers on the premises when – for no apparent reason – fire broke out on the 11th floor. Those closest to the exits – about 50 people – ran out with their clothes and hair on fire: they were more fortunate than many because, within seconds, everyone else inside the building had been cut off.

As the flames spread upwards, many people hurried upstairs. With the benefit of hindsight, this was a fatal error, but at the time it must have seemed the only rational thing to do. Those who had already been to the top of the building would have known that the highest levels were still unaffected by fire; others would have felt instinctively that it was too risky to try to get down through the fire to the ground floor. But the problem with this course of action was that the fire ladders could not reach more than halfway up the building.

At the time, São Paulo – a city of eight million people – had only 20 fire stations. Although the alarm was raised quickly there were insufficient fire tenders for the task and those that did answer the call were delayed by traffic jams and the crowds that had gathered in the surrounding streets to watch the blaze.

Meanwhile, the fire had taken hold of the Joelma Building, which was built of a cocktail of flammable materials. Many of the people still inside climbed out onto window ledges, desperately shouting for help. As the flames crept up on them, they faced a terrible choice between jumping and being burned to death.

When the rescue services finally arrived, they did all they could in the circumstances, and one brave fireman rescued 18 people whom he helped to safety along ropes which had been shot from nearby buildings. Eventually, after four hours, the flames were brought under control, but by then 227 people had died and 250 others had been seriously burned or injured in other ways. Despite police investigations, the precise cause of the fire was never established.

HOTEL FIRE, SEOUL, SOUTH KOREA

NOVEMBER 3, 1974

Below: An aerial view of downtown Seoul, where the hotel was situated. The nightclub, where most of the dead were trapped, was on the sixth floor of the seven-storey building.

Eighty-eight people were killed and another 30 seriously injured in a fire that swept through a hotel in the eastern part of Seoul, the South Korean capital, during the early hours of a Sunday morning. The seven-storey building had a nightclub on its sixth floor, and most of the dead were customers who were trapped inside it because the doors had been locked to prevent them leaving before they had paid their bills.

The blaze began when a hotel guest fell asleep while smoking in bed and the cigarette set fire to the mattress. By the time the fire was noticed it had taken a firm hold – it eventually raged for three hours before

firemen brought it under control. By that time it had raced through the hotel and gutted the top two floors of the building.

Sixty-four bodies were recovered from the nightclub where more than 200 customers, mostly young people, had been dancing. Of the other victims, 13 were hotel guests who burned or were suffocated to death in their rooms, eight jumped to their deaths from upstairs windows, and three were found dead on the roof.

Seoul city authorities later removed the director of the regional office of public hygiene from his post on the grounds of negligence because the nightclub, which had been within his jurisdiction, had failed to close at 0200 hours as required by law.

ALEXANDRA PALACE, LONDON, ENGLAND

JULY 10, 1980

Much of the magnificent Alexandra Palace in north London was destroyed by a fire which started accidentally in the organ loft shortly after workmen had begun preliminary restoration of the famous Henry Willis instrument inside it. No one was seriously injured in the blaze, but millions of pounds' worth of damage were caused and for some time it was uncertain whether the site could be rebuilt or if it would have to be flattened and covered with grass.

Despite its name, Alexandra Palace was not a royal residence but an exhibition building. Occupying seven acres (2.8 hectares), it featured Europe's largest hall – a distinction it retained right up until the day it was destroyed – a concert room, reading room, theater, and offices. It had burned down once before, just over a fortnight after it originally opened in 1873, when a red-hot coal fell from a workman's brazier, but it was rebuilt and was back in operation by 1875.

Alexandra Palace was never entirely successful as an exhibition center as most businesses continued to prefer the Crystal Palace in south London. But the extensive potential office space in Alexandra Palace and the fact that it was built on some of the highest ground in London made it attractive to the BBC's fledgling television service. In 1936 the company acquired part of it for television studios and a transmitter, and it was from here, on August 26 the same year, that the world's first television broadcast was made.

By the time of the fire, although the BBC's main television centre had moved to west London, "Ally Pally" – as it was generally called – still contained the television studios of the Open University.

Left: Smoke pours from Alexandra Palace as firemen make desperate efforts to contain the blaze.

Right: The wreck of the great exhibition hall, which had been constructed in metal and glass in imitation of the Crystal Palace.

The fire was first spotted by a police patrol flying past in a helicopter on routine surveillance duty above the British capital. It spread quickly and destroyed at least 60 percent of the complex. More than 200 firemen rushed to the scene and fought the blaze but much of the Palace was destroyed, along with sound equipment worth more than £250,000 ($400,000) which had recently been brought in for a planned jazz festival. About 350 BBC staff were evacuated.

The overall glass roof of the great exhibition hall collapsed in a series of explosions, buckling the metal supports and sending two million square feet (186 thousand sq m) of glass crashing to the floor. A pall of smoke rose high into the air and could be seen in central London, six miles (10km) away.

After enormous efforts to raise the finance, Alexandra Palace was partially restored and the new complex houses exhibition and banqueting halls and an ice rink.

GRAND HOTEL, LAS VEGAS, USA

NOVEMBER 21, 1980

One hundred people were burned to death or asphyxiated and more than 600 injured, many of them seriously, when fire swept through the 26-storey MGM Grand Hotel in Las Vegas, Nevada, USA. The blaze sent noxious smoke billowing through most of the 2000 rooms where many of the 3500 guests were asleep.

The fire started at about 0700 hours in the kitchen of the ground floor restaurant. Within moments, the adjacent casino was ablaze throughout its 147-yard (134m) length. The flames knocked out the hotel's electrical circuits so rapidly that the automatic fire alarms did not go off. Later, when guests telephoned reception for instructions they could not get through because the switchboard had also been put out of action. After the fire was discovered, no one thought to set off the manually operated alarms – even if they had been activated they would have been of little benefit because only three floors of the hotel had their own sprinkler systems. Although this may seem shocking with hindsight, it did not violate Las Vegas fire regulations at the time.

The smoke rose unchecked up the building through stair wells and lift shafts. As it spread it fed off plastic furnishings and became ever more lethal to inhale.

Below: The Las Vegas firefighting services tackle the fire at the Grand Hotel. The fire started early in the morning on the ground floor, and destroyed the electrical circuits so that the fire alarms did not ring.

Right: At the height of the fire a great cloud of black smoke and poisonous fumes from the burning furnishings rose above the hotel. A helicopter hovers on the left of the picture, seeking an opportunity to rescue hotel guests from the roof or balconies.

When it reached the upper floors, many of the guests remained uncertain what to do: despite the apparent danger, the absence of any alarm engendered a false sense of security. As the fumes intensified the guests at last recognized the danger they were in. The ensuing scenes of panic were described by a man who watched the tragedy from a hotel across the street as "sheer bedlam". Smoke had now enveloped nearly all the building, and guests waved sheets or threw chairs and tables through the windows of their rooms in a desperate attempt to get fresh air to breathe.

Six helicopters from a nearby US Air Force base were scrambled and rescued many of the guests by picking them off the balconies of their rooms and from the roof. Meanwhile, police helicopters circled the hotel pleading with guests through bullhorns not to jump. One woman did jump and was killed.

At street level, those who had been near the main exit or had managed to reach it swarmed out of the hotel in frightened droves. One witness described how the casino girls and dealers rushed away from the inferno "with cash drawers in their hands stuffing chips in their pockets".

Most of those who died were trapped on the upper floors, far beyond the reach of the fire brigade's ladders, which extended only nine storeys. When the flames were eventually brought under control, firemen began to evacuate the building floor by floor, using window-cleaners' platforms to winch people to safety.

Left: Firemen encourage a hotel guest to esape down one of their ladders, which unfortunately only extended as far as the ninth storey. Other guests were rescued in window cleaners' platforms.

STATUTO CINEMA, TURIN, ITALY
FEBRUARY 13, 1983

Right: A body is carried out of the Statuto cinema after the fire that killed 74 people. The rear emergency exits were found to be locked, and the manager of the cinema was subsequently arrested.

Seventy-four people were killed when fire swept through the Statuto Cinema in the centre of Turin, Italy. There were at first thought to be only 37 dead, but firemen later discovered the same number of bodies in the upper gallery and in the upstairs toilets, where they had been suffocated by smoke fumes.

The fire started in the stalls and spread quickly, engulfing seats with plastic covers from which deadly smoke billowed up into the gallery. There was at the time no clear legislation in Italy to prevent the use of upholstery which gave off toxic fumes when hot. This helps to explain why the smoke was so bad that firemen were still having to wear breathing apparatus several hours after the blaze had been brought under control. Although people from the stalls were killed – many in the stampede to escape – the survivors had all been sitting on the ground floor, close to where the fire broke out. Everyone upstairs died.

Below: Most of the victims of the fire were given an official funeral in Turin's cathedral attended by the President of Italy.

Police said that there was no evidence of arson and that the blaze had probably been started accidentally by one of three things: a burning cigarette end, an electrical short circuit, or a firework set off as a joke – the tragedy occurred on the Sunday two days before Shrove Tuesday and fireworks are always popular at this time of year as Italians celebrate the carnival at the beginning of Lent.

Whatever started the fire, it would almost certainly have caused fewer deaths if the attendants had been on duty at the rear emergency exits, as they should have been. In their absence, the back doors had been locked to prevent latecomers getting in without paying. This meant that nobody could get out that way, and when the fire brigade arrived they had to break their way in with axes.

Of the remaining members of the audience in the 1070-seat cinema, most escaped unscathed: only three people were injured. Nearly all the victims were young: the average age was only 25 and the youngest were a boy aged 11 and a girl aged seven.

Among the dead was Giacomo Fracchia, aged 20. He was a Cuirassier – one of the Italian army's ceremonial guards – and that is one of the reasons why all those killed in the fire were offered an official funeral in Turin Cathedral after a funeral Mass celebrated by the Cardinal Archbishop of the city and attended by the President of Italy. This honor was angrily turned down by 15 of the other victims' families – many of whom were poor economic migrants from the south of the country – who condemned it as ostentatious political interference in private grief.

YORK MINSTER, YORK, ENGLAND

JULY 9, 1984

Above: Although the fire gutted the south transept of the cathedral, the medieval stained glass windows escaped untouched, including the beautiful circular rose window.

A bolt of lightning during an electrical storm in the summer of 1984 struck one of the pinnacles on top of York Minster and started a fire that destroyed nearly all the south transept, causing damage worth over £1 million ($1.6 million). Despite the enormous destruction, many people were grateful that the disaster had not been much worse – no one was hurt, and the greater part of Europe's largest Gothic cathedral remained unscathed.

In the early evening of July 8, an electrical storm raged over York and local people noticed that flashes of lightning appeared to play particularly about the roof of the Minster. The blaze was first spotted at 0230 hours in the early hours of the next day. The cathedral was fully protected against lightning and had numerous fire detectors throughout the concourse and lightning conductors on its pinnacles. Nevertheless, the sheer speed of the spread of the flames defeated all attempts to extinguish them, even after the rapid arrival of fire engines from nearby Northallerton.

The blaze was intensified by the cathedral's old, dry timbers and lead roof. It took almost three hours to bring the fire under control, and by then the ancient roof beams and plaster vaults of the transept (the part of the cathedral running at right angles to the nave) had been reduced to a smoldering mass of debris on the floor. In the morning light it was discovered that the high gable on the south wall of the transept was no longer supported by the roof.

Despite the horrendous damage, there was universal joy that the fire had been put out before it had reached the Minster's world-renowned collection of stained glass, particularly the unique 15th-century rose window. Many of the cathedral's treasures were saved by teams of clergy who ran relays and braved fire and showers of molten lead to salvage priceless artefacts. Only when the roof beams gave way did they give up. At the height of the blaze, a Minster clergyman and his wife dashed into the cathedral and rescued valuable items from the high altar before they were told firmly by firemen that they must leave.

Gossip at the time linked the fire to the recent consecration as Bishop of Durham of the Right Reverend David Jenkins, a controversial liberal clergyman – some suspected arson by protesters against his appointment, while others thought it was divine intervention, an act of God. Police quickly ruled out the former, while of the latter Dr Robert Runcie, Archbishop of Canterbury – who was in York at the time for a General Synod – said "it seems absolutely miraculous that the fire was confined to the transept. York Minster has risen before and it will rise again." He also quoted the words of the Chief Fire Officer: "The Lord was on our side as we battled with those flames, and every man in my brigade knew they were doing something special by saving York Minster."

Below: In the aftermath of the fire that destroyed the roof of the south transept, experts check on the damage.

BRADFORD CITY FOOTBALL STADIUM, ENGLAND

MAY 11, 1985

Fifty-six people were burned to death, 70 more detained in the hospital with severe burns, and a further 211 supporters and police were injured when a timber stand caught fire at Bradford City's Valley Parade ground during an end-of-season game. The fire broke out just before half time beneath wooden tip-up seats three rows from the back of Block G during the final home league match of the season against Lincoln City.

The game was fairly well attended, because Bradford had just ensured promotion from the old English Third Division, and many fans had come to celebrate. The fire began amid rubbish that had accumulated beneath the stand over a long period and had never been swept up. The felt and wood roof, which was tinder-dry, fed the flames that rapidly engulfed the structure. When the fire was first noticed, there were a few tongues of flame licking the base of a row of seats. Within two minutes it had spread the entire length of the stand, moving faster than grown men could run.

Most of the victims were trapped in the stand itself. Many of the men, women, and young children who died were so badly mutilated that they could be identified only from dental records. The first to perish were those who tried to reach the back of the stand; of those who fled onto the pitch, most were saved. At least 15 bodies were found in a walkway 4 feet (1.3m) wide which ran along the entire length of the back of the stand.

A dozen bodies were found in clusters of two or three lying against six of the exits. They had been crushed to death as they desperately attempted to crawl out under turnstiles which had been locked to prevent latecomers getting in without paying. To make matters worse, there were no fire extinguishers in this part of the ground: they had been removed and stored in a room in the clubhouse because during previous games they been set off and used as missiles by unruly fans. The Chief Fire Officer of West Yorkshire, interviewed in *The Times*, said that as far as he knew there had never been a fire inspection at the ground because under English law the Fire Brigade was not empowered to carry one out on private property.

Right: An aerial view of Bradford football stadium showing the burning stand. The fire was fanned by a draught of air from the back when someone opened a door.

Above: *The stand quickly became an inferno. Most of the people who jumped onto the pitch escaped, but those who tried to get out at the back found the turnstiles locked.*

One spectator said: "We all thought it would be out in a few minutes. Everyone was telling us not to panic." Another survivor reported: "We could see the flames creeping along the bottom of the seats, then it seemed that someone opened a door at the back to let people out. There was a northerly breeze, which created a tunnel of wind, and it was like a furnace. People panicked and were rushing onto the pitch. I went across to help people into the ambulances and there were men with their hair burnt off and their faces burned. There were children walking around with burns on their hands."

Left: *Fans watch the stand burn from the comparative safety of the pitch. In all 56 people died in the disaster and many more were severely burned, or otherwise injured, and kept in the hospital.*

HAMPTON COURT PALACE, LONDON, ENGLAND

MARCH 31, 1986

Above: The fire at Hampton Court Palace started in one of the "grace and favor" apartments on the top floor.

A fire that devastated the Cartoon Gallery of Hampton Court Palace, the historic English royal residence on the outskirts of London, killed a general's widow and caused damage worth more than £1 million ($1.6 million).

The fire broke out upstairs in the Palace's south wing, designed by Sir Christopher Wren, one of the greatest English architects. The wing housed the Cartoon Gallery, named for the Raphael drawings that had been brought to England by King Charles I and were displayed there until the mid-19th century when they were removed to the Victoria and Albert Museum.

The upper floor of this wing was residential, a "grace and favor" apartment occupied by Lady Gale,

aged 86, the widow of General Sir Richard Gale, who in the 1950s had been Commander-in-Chief of the British Army of the Rhine. Lady Gale had been in the habit of reading by candlelight, and this is thought to have been the cause of the disaster. Palace staff later revealed that they had been concerned for some time at Lady Gale's increasing inability to fend for herself. One aide was reported as saying: "She was in the habit of taking a drink at night by candlelight and falling asleep sometimes with the candle still burning. Some of the ladies had feared a fire might start."

The fire probably broke out at about 0230 hours but went undetected until 0530 hours, when the alarms went off. Although Hampton Court Palace had fire extinguishers, there was no sprinkler system because

it was feared it might go off accidentally and damage some of the priceless furnishings and paintings.

The emergency services were summoned at 0545, by which time a huge pall of smoke could be seen more than two miles (3km) away. Six other elderly residents – the widows of generals, diplomats, and former colonial service officials – were woken immediately and moved out of their top floor apartments to safety. Over 120 firemen from all over London and Surrey were mustered to fight the blaze. Tight security protecting the Palace treasures meant that they had to smash their way with pickaxes through the Cartoon Gallery's barred and reinforced doors.

Not long afterwards the roof of the building collapsed and crashed onto the Cartoon Gallery 40 feet (12m) below. The smoke was appallingly thick. There was an enormous amount of timber and other debris falling all the time and it was impossible to see or hear anything through the glare and noise of the inferno.

Firefighters rescued everything that was portable, but they were too late to save two valuable paintings, along with much furniture and oak panelling. Two other famous paintings – "The Field of the Cloth of Gold" and a portrait of King Henry VIII – were blackened by smoke and drenched with water from the firemen's hoses, but they were salvageable and were taken at once to the restorers.

Above: *Despite the efforts of the firefighters, much of the south wing of the Palace was destroyed.*

Right: *Although the Tudor part of the Palace (seen on the left here) escaped the fire, half of Sir Christopher Wren's 17th-century south wing (in the foreground) was devastated, including its ancient roof timbers.*

WINDSOR CASTLE, WINDSOR, ENGLAND

NOVEMBER 20, 1992

Art treasures beyond price were destroyed when a disastrous fire broke out in Queen Elizabeth II's private chapel in Windsor Castle where electrical rewiring work had been in progress. The blaze raged for seven hours and wrecked some of the most beautiful state apartments in the castle including St George's Hall, the scene of many magnificent banquets, which lost its fine timber roof and was gutted.

The fire was first spotted by picture restorers who were packing paintings to be stored during the latest stage of a refurbishment project which had been going on since 1989. Someone went for a fire extinguisher, but by the time he got one it was plain that the fire was

serious. By now, members of the public walking past the northeast corner of the castle noticed a thin line of white smoke rising from behind the battlements. The alarm was raised at 1137 hours and at 1148 ten fire engines arrived just as the smoke turned to black – a reliable sign that the blaze had taken firm hold. As soon as the firemen in attendance realized the size of the fire, they called for reinforcements – within an hour 35 appliances had rushed to the scene from all over Berkshire and the neighboring counties of Buckinghamshire, Oxfordshire, Surrey, and London.

While firemen hosed the flames, teams of volunteers carried priceless works of art out of the inferno. Among them was Prince Andrew, Duke of York, who had been one of the first to arrive at the scene. Human

Above: The scene from Windsor Great Park, as dark smoke belches out of the castle.

One man who had been working in the dining room only a few yards from the private chapel tried to rescue some paintings, but he had to give up when he suffered burns to his hands. Later, speaking from a hospital bed, he said he had originally wanted to put out the fire but when he went to the entrance to the chapel "it was an inferno. The curtains were on fire and the walls were burning. It was all going up."

The fire leaped through the roof of the castle buildings and onlookers watched helplessly as lead in the roof melted and glass windows came crashing down. Every time the firemen got close, it flared up again and drove them back. At the height of the blaze, lorryloads of Life Guards arrived to join the rescue operation.

By the time the fire was put out, the damage was devastating. Eight valuable and historic paintings were beyond repair, all of them from the private chapel, most of the roof was destroyed and the structure of the building seriously weakened. Prince Andrew described the scene as "a very nasty mess, full of acrid smoke, warm and very wet". Although there was no loss of life and few injuries, one indirect victim of the Windsor

Above: Firemen tackling the blaze from high vantage points.

Right: The restoration of the state apartments of Windsor Castle cost many millions of pounds, and also gave employment to many highly skilled craftsmen.

chains passed furniture out into Engine Court and the castle courtyard soon became filled with a vast collection of ornate sofas, cabinets, and lampstands. Some items were loaded immediately into the moving vans which had come to collect the paintings, but many were left to stand for hours in the damp air.

conflagration was Christopher Lloyd, surveyor of the Queen's pictures, who was taken to hospital later that day with a suspected heart attack.

Restoration of the fire-damaged parts of Windsor Castle and 100 of its paintings was completed in late 1997 at a cost of £37 million ($60 million).

DUSSELDORF AIRPORT, GERMANY

APRIL 11, 1996

Left: A small fire that started in a florist's shop on the concourse of Düsseldorf airport turned into a major disaster when it melted dangerous materials that produced toxic fumes.

Sixteen people were killed and 150 injured when fire broke out in a flower shop on one of the concourses of Düsseldorf International Airport. Düsseldorf is the main point of entry to the industrial Ruhr and, after Frankfurt-am-Main, its airport is the second busiest in Germany.

One of the worst aspects of this tragedy was that the fire itself was not particularly serious or life-threatening. The problem was the effect of intense heat on materials which, though flame-resistant, were nevertheless extremely dangerous because they melted and belched highly toxic gases into a confined space.

German police reported that many of the deaths were caused by inhaling the poisonous fumes emitted from molten plastic. Nine of the victims – a police officer, seven women and a small child – were found asphyxiated in one of the elevators. The other seven bodies were found in the lavatories and in the Air France lounge – they too had all been suffocated.

The blaze started at about 1625 hours in Terminal A, the main arrivals hall for domestic and international flights of the German airline Lufthansa. Sparks were seen flying out of a ventilation grille above the florist's stall, and it is believed that these may have come from the power drill of a maintenance mechanic working

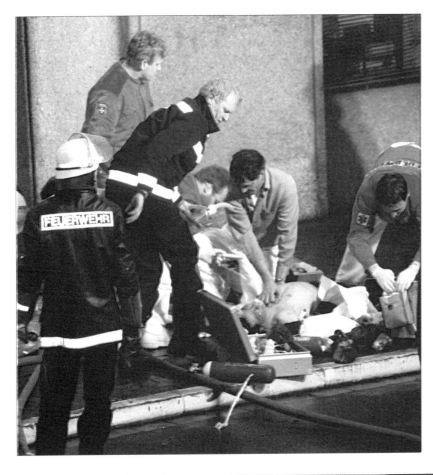

above the false ceiling. The sparks quickly took hold of the plastic around the grille and became a fire which spread rapidly, sending bitter, choking smoke through ventilation shafts and passageways to many other parts of the airport.

The fire brigade was called immediately and the airport swung into its much-practised security drill. As soon as the alarm sounded, all aircraft on the tarmac were towed as far away from the terminal as possible. The control tower radioed incoming flights with instructions to divert to Konrad Adenaeur Airport, 35 miles (56km) to the north, which serves Cologne and Bonn. Passengers in the departures lounge who had been unaffected by the fire were taken immediately by coach to other airports.

Meanwhile, in the terminal building, smoke had spread rapidly through air-conditioning conduits – both the arrivals and departures halls were now enveloped in a pall of smoke – and the fire had worked its way down to the rail station beneath the terminal. Rescue teams had to wear breathing apparatus as they groped their way through the smoke-filled ruins.

Although everyone in the airport had been instructed to evacuate as soon as the alarm had been raised, there was still an unexpectedly high number of casualties. This is thought to have been because people panicked and forgot that they were supposed to head straight for the emergency exits – this explains why there were so many deaths in the elevator.

Above:
Paramedics
attend to one of
the injured.

Right: Even
though the
emergency
services were
quickly on the
scene, there was a
high number of
casualties due to
the poisonous
smoke that filled
the airport.

UNDERGROUND FIRES

There are few places where people feel more at risk than beneath the surface of the earth. Although there are well-established psychological reasons for this fear, the dangers are undeniably real. This is especially true in mines, where the physical labor is tough and often carried out in adverse conditions. The miner's lot has often been made even more dangerous by inadequate safety provisions. The 1913 disaster at Sengenhydd in Wales was one of many mining tragedies that might never have happened if safety provisions had been adequate.

Fire in an underground passage – whether it be a coal mine or a subway tunnel – is concentrated by its confined surroundings. While a blaze above ground may spread over a wide area, it may also dissipate itself and become less of a danger. Below ground it is the monarch of all it encounters – the air is hot and often full of combustible gases; at the deepest levels, there is greatly increased air pressure and sparks may occur spontaneously. If one of these bursts into flame, all the available oxygen in the passage will be burnt up and the fire will rush off in search of further supplies. This will lead it to the surface, often with disastrous consequences such as those at Farmington, West Virginia, USA, in 1968. The same effect – which is sometimes known as flashover – was also created in the 1987 fire at King's Cross Underground station in London, England.

Right: The entrance to King's Cross Underground station on the night of November 18, 1987, when a wooden escalator in the station caught fire, killing 30 people.

SENGENHYDD MINE, WALES

OCTOBER 14, 1913

Britain's worst coal mining disaster was caused by the fire which followed a gas explosion deep below ground at the Universal Colliery, Sengenhydd, South Wales. Although 500 miners were brought up alive, 439 others were killed. The initial blast was so loud that – despite being underground – it was still clearly audible 11 miles (18km) away in Cardiff.

From the mid-19th century onwards, when coal became the lynchpin of the British economy, Wales had a reputation for having the best seams and the worst mines. The pits were dangerous partly because they were dug so deep and partly because the seams they exploited had a high content of explosive gas, particularly firedamp, a form of methane.

Although the Sengenhydd mine was a comparatively recent working – it had been fully opened only in 1896 – it had already been the scene of a major tragedy: in May 1901 a large methane explosion had killed all but one of the 82 men working below ground. Nevertheless, the mine was also one of the most

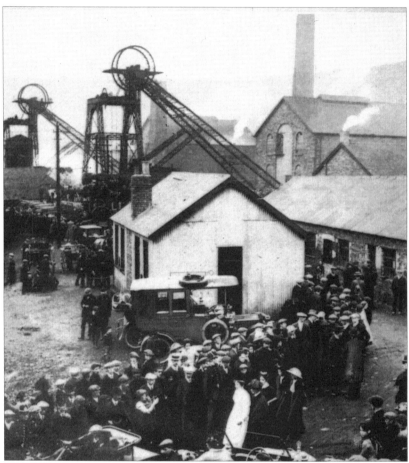

productive for its size: by 1913, Sengenhydd was producing about 1800 tons of coal every day.

Because of the earlier tragedy, the Sengenhydd pit was examined regularly for firedamp, and indeed it was checked first thing on the morning of Tuesday, October 14, before the early shift went down at 0600 hours. At 0810 hours, however, a huge explosion ripped through the mine and blocked the adit (entrance) with rock and debris. The pit's own rescue crew cleared the rubble and went down immediately, but when they reached the main underground working, they found that half the pit – and half the miners – were cut off by a wall of fire.

Although the rescue teams quickly realized that they needed outside assistance, the fire brigade was unaccountably not called out for nearly two hours and the long delay is believed to have been one of the major contributory factors to the extent of this tragedy.

By the end of the day, rescue teams had found no survivors and only 12 bodies had been removed from

Above: Anxious families gather at the pit head as news of the disaster spreads around the mining village.

Left: The scene at Sengenhydd mine after the explosion that fatally trapped 439 miners.

Right: The underground explosion ripped apart the gear at the head of the pit. Immediately afterwards one half of the mine erupted in a mass of flames.

the mine. The following morning the search resumed and 18 men were found alive in one small area. Later, they pulled out an unconscious boy who was revived after two hours of artificial respiration.

It was several more days before all the miners who had been down the pit were accounted for. When the extent of the tragedy became known, grief swept the nation. There was a government inquiry which found that, despite numerous safety precautions, the mine remained appallingly dangerous. Seam walls and ceilings which should have been swept regularly were covered in flammable coal dust. Newly introduced signaling equipment was run by batteries and the sparks from them could have ignited the firedamp. The steam fan which circulated air through the mine was also a hazard and possibly one of the causes of the tragedy because, unlike the ventilation systems in other pits, it could not be instantly reversed to stem the flow of flame-fanning air. The Sengenhydd Colliery manager was eventually brought to court and fined £24 – local people bitterly remarked that this was about one shilling per dead miner.

FARMINGTON, WEST VIRGINIA, USA

NOVEMBER 20, 1968

Seventy-eight men died after a series of methane gas explosions sparked terrible fires below ground in the Consol No. 9 coal mine near Farmington, 10 miles (16 km) outside Monongay, West Virginia, USA.

The shallow mine extended 8 miles (13 km) from east to west and six miles (9.5 km) from north to south through an underground coal seam between the small towns of Farmington and Mannington. Below the excavations lay a rich but still untapped reservoir of oil and natural gas.

At about 0540 hours on a winter's morning, one large underground explosion and three secondary blasts sent massive shock waves through the mine and up to the surface. The most seriously damaged building at the pit head was the lamphouse, a store room in which were kept not only the miners' lamps but also the one complete list of the names of those on shift at the time. Of the men who had gone to work 600 feet (180m) underground at midnight, 21 were quickly hauled to safety. The rest, however, remained unidentified until frantic calls to the their homes enabled a new register to be compiled. By 0800 hours, when the shift was due to end, it had been established that there had been 99 men in the mine, and that 78 of them were unaccounted for.

Hours after the main explosion, dense black smoke from the fire still rose in a column above one of the ten main adits (entrances) to the mine. Teams of rescuers stood ready at the other nine entrances but were not allowed to go down at once for fear of further explosions. During the day engineers put bricks and concrete over two of the ventilation shafts in an attempt to direct the flow of air away from the fire and towards the area in which it was thought most likely that any survivors might have taken refuge.

But at 2200 hours that evening, another blast of methane gas blew out the seals and flames again roared through the wrecked entrances to the mine. Rescue workers now began to think it would be days or even weeks before they could go down. The only hope for the trapped men was if they had managed to

Left: Clouds of smoke billow from the Llewellyn Portal of the Consol No. 9 coal mine on November 20, 1968, after a series of massive explosions started fires in the mine that were to trap and kill 78 miners.

Right: A miner tests the air for gas. It was thought to be explosions of methane gas that started the disastrous fires that swept through the Consol mine.

escape into an area near where the 21 survivors had been found. But there were now only two working ventilators and it was doubtful if the men could have reached the areas these fans were supplying.

Then, during the night, there was a further explosion and the fire turned back towards where the men were trapped. More smoke belched out from the main shaft. The only way to stop the fire was to starve it completely of air, but to do so would also kill any

survivors. Ventilation holes were drilled into the ground directly above the chambers in which the men were thought to be. Sensors suggested that this part of the mine was high in methane and low in oxygen, but could still have supported life.

Nevertheless, no contact with the trapped miners was ever made. On November 30, hope was abandoned and the mine was finally sealed with its 78 victims entombed for ever.

THE KELLOGG MINE, IDAHO, USA

MAY 2, 1972

Right: Smoke pours out of the Sunshine silver mine at Kellogg, Idaho, after a fire started below ground in one of the worked-out seams.

All mining is hazardous, and the deeper the mine the greater the danger. The Sunshine Mine at Kellogg in the hills of Idaho, USA, is one of the deepest excavations in the world. It has been mined extensively for its silver, a precious native element that generally forms in long, thin veins. These deposits may extend for great distances under ground, and over many years the excavation of the seams at the Kellogg mine has created a labyrinthine warren of diggings, some of which are so deep that miners can stay down there for no longer than 30 minutes at a time.

The fire that killed 91 men at the Sunshine Mine started in one of the many worked-out parts of the mine, 3700 feet (1100m) below ground. At depths like these, there is greatly increased pressure and temperatures typically in excess of 100°F (38°C). In such conditions, sparks may be created for no apparent reason. This phenomenon, known as spontaneous combustion, is thought to have happened at the Sunshine Mine at midday on May 2, setting fire to one of the supporting timbers. The fire spread quickly, but the smoke outran it into the ventilation shafts.

Throughout the rest of the day, a column of thick white smoke belched out of the mine's main exhaust stack at the pit head. Rescue teams wearing oxygen masks went down immediately to search for survivors in the smoky darkness, while engineers set about sealing off empty shafts to prevent the fire from spreading even further. Once the location of the fire had been identified, fresh air was pumped down into nearby parts of the mine to help any miners who might have taken refuge in neighboring galleries.

Many miners were brought out safely, but the bodies of 24 men were soon found lying at the bottom of the main elevator shaft. These victims included the elevator operators – one of the worst aspects of this tragedy was that no one else below ground knew how to operate the elevators and they could not be controlled

Right: On May 9, seven days after the outbreak of fire, an official from the Bureau of Mines prepares to ride a steel capsule down to the level where the fire started.

from ground level. It was thought that the remainder of the shift who were unaccounted for might have fled to safety in another part of the mine – but the mine contained hundreds of miles of tunnels and the question was, where were they? Further teams of rescuers were lowered down the main shaft in a capsule on a steel cable.

The search continued for a week, by the end of which 47 bodies had been recovered. Hope was fading, when rescuers found two men still alive and in good health 4800 feet (1440m) below ground. They had survived on the pumped-in air and by eating the packed lunches of the men who had died. This discovery raised expectations among relatives at the pit head, but shortly afterwards a massive cave-in severed lines carrying compressed air. No one else came out alive.

The subsequent inquiry slammed the safety measures at the Sunshine Mine, which had provided inadequate training and no protective chemical masks.

Below: A young miner, Tom Wilkenson, is brought out of the mine alive and well seven days after the fire started. He and another miner survived on the packed lunches of their dead workmates in an air pocket of pumped-in air.

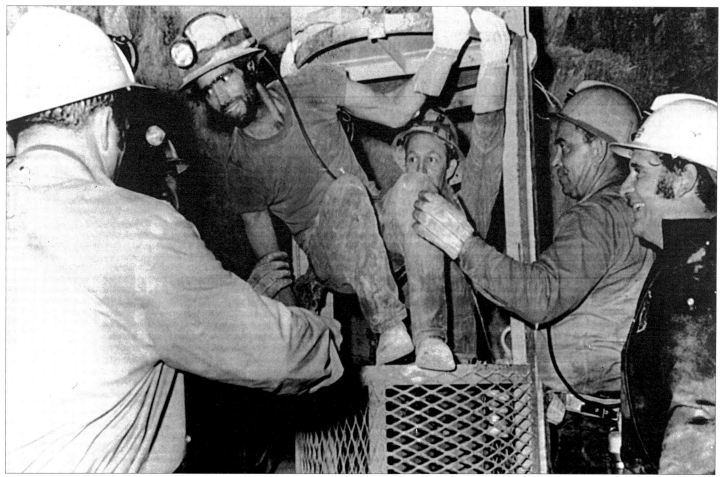

ALCALA 20 DISCO, MADRID, SPAIN

DECEMBER 17, 1983

Eighty-three young people were killed in the early hours of the morning when fire ripped through Alcalà 20, an underground discothèque near Puerta del Sol in central Madrid, Spain. Most of the dead were either asphyxiated or trampled under foot. The fire began at about 0445 hours when the disco was about to close and the rock music had been turned off. In contrast to many fatal fires in public places, the club was not overcrowded – there were only about 600 people in a building licensed to hold 900. But, as the subsequent investigation disclosed, this was one of the few things that could be said in favor of the place – in almost every other particular, Alcalà 20 was a fire prevention officer's worst nightmare.

One survivor said that the first he knew about the fire was when he saw "a flame leap out of the stage curtains. Within seconds there were fumes, hardly letting you breathe. That is when the stampede started, with hundreds of people trying to escape. I tried to grab the hands of some girls I saw being trampled underfoot, but it was like an unstoppable avalanche."

Another survivor spoke of how he had groped his way through the smoke looking for the ground floor exit but had been unable to find it because it was so badly signposted. He finally managed to clamber up to street level through a ventilator shaft, the protective glass at the top of which had apparently been smashed by someone escaping ahead of him. Many of those who did reach the exit ended up in a crush because the doors were too small to release all the people inside in time – it was just inside the main entrance that the rescue services eventually found the greatest number of trampled bodies.

Situated in the refurbished basement of an old theatre, the Alcalà 20 discothèque had opened only three months previously. The conversion of the premises had been approved by all the relevant Spanish authorities, including the Madrid College of Architects and inspectors from the Industry Ministry.

After the tragedy, in response to criticism of locating such a public venue below ground level, Madrid's Civil Governor, Señor José Rodriguez, said: "Most

Left: The fire-damaged entrance to the Alcalà disco. In the stampede to get out, the doors proved to be too small and many trampled bodies were found near the exit.

Right: The scene in the disco after the fire. Lights on the dance floor short-circuited and within minutes the underground disco was an inferno.

discothèques all over the world so far as I know are underground because of the noise of the music."

It was subsequently discovered that the fire had probably been started by an electrical short circuit in the lights on the dance floor. The poisonous fumes had been given off from plastic curtains, wall hangings, and upholstery. Although there was a brief period during which the fire might possibly have been brought under control, the club's 10 fire extinguishers were either too difficult to operate or did not work at all.

Right: Firemen search through the debris of the gutted dance hall, looking for bodies of victims killed by the fire.

KING'S CROSS UNDERGROUND STATION, LONDON, ENGLAND

NOVEMBER 18, 1987

Above: Firemen inspect the damage after the fire at King's Cross Underground station that killed 30 passengers at the height of the evening rush hour.

When a 48-year-old wooden escalator caught fire at the Piccadilly Line exit from King's Cross, London's busiest Underground station, it was during the evening rush hour. In the resulting blaze 30 commuters were burned to death.

The blaze began when fluff under the escalator caught fire, possibly from a discarded match or cigarette end. The result was the type of fire known as a flashover – a searing wall of flame that rushed from the foot of the moving walkway to the booking hall upstairs, 50 feet (15m) below street level. PC Stephen Hanson, a London Transport policeman on duty that night, described it as "a shock wave of fire" that knocked him off his feet.

Assistant Chief Fire Officer Joe Kennedy, who was in charge of operations on the night, described the blaze as "one of the worst kind of situations that fire fighters have to face. Because of the concrete tunnels, the heat generated by the fire was not released." Testimony to the ferocity of the blaze is that there were so few survivors: the fire took almost everyone it encountered.

All but one of the victims had been downstairs on or near the platforms when the fire was first detected. They had then tried to reach safety at ground level, but the fire – fanned by the draught of passing trains – pursued them up the escalator and killed them in the booking hall. The other fatal casualty was Station Officer Colin Townley of Red Watch at Soho Fire Station, who died fighting the blaze.

The inquiry into the King's Cross fire caused great disquiet about safety standards on the Underground system. One revelation was that passengers had seen smoke coming from the same escalator earlier that day – this had been reported to London Underground staff, but the warnings had gone unheeded. Worse, there was no sprinkler system on the station.

There was further controversy about the amount of training London Underground staff were given to combat such emergencies. London Regional Transport, the administrative body in charge of the station, maintained that "all staff go through two and a half days' emergency training and have to take part in special local training when they move to a new station." Employees at King's Cross, however, said that they had been given no formal training whatever, and

Above: The remains of the escalators from the Piccadilly Line after the flashover fire gutted them.

Left: The booking hall in the underground concourse at the station on the morning after the fire.

the question of how to organize an evacuation in the event of a fire had never been raised, nor had there ever been a fire drill practice. One railman said that in 10 years' service at the station he had only been given a few minutes' instruction in using a fire extinguisher.

There were two important consequences of the King's Cross disaster – one was that wooden escalators were quickly phased out of the London Underground system; the other was that smoking was banned throughout the system, both on platforms and on trains.

One male victim of the King's Cross fire has never been identified. A decade after the event, an artist's impression of his reconstructed face was shown to the public in the hope he might yet be recognized.

SUBWAY TRAIN, BAKU, AZERBAIJAN

OCTOBER 29, 1995

Left: Narimanov underground station in Baku. A fire broke out in the tunnel between Narimanov and the next station along the line, Ulduz, during the evening rush hour.

More than 300 people died and 270 were injured, 62 of them seriously, when a crowded subway train caught fire while it was trapped in a tunnel in Baku, the capital of Azerbaijan. The main causes of death were asphyxiation and burns, but several of the victims were electrocuted as they tried to escape along the track to the nearest station.

The five-car train was packed with commuters when it juddered to a halt between Ulduz and Narimanov stations during the Saturday evening rush hour. In an instant, all the lights went out and the carriages began to fill with smoke from a fire that had already started in the tunnel. Passengers immediately began trying to escape, but the sliding doors remained firmly shut. They then attempted to break the windows, but the people were so tightly packed in the carriages that they could not get enough of a swing at the glass to break it.

Both the fire and the short circuit which stopped the train were caused by sparks from a high-voltage cable in the tunnel which had set light to the insulating material in which it was encased. This wrapping was made of PVC, which gives off acrid and highly poisonous fumes when it melts. Because it was so dangerous, insulation of this type had been removed from all

Right: A street market in Baku, the capital of Azerbaijan. Part of the former Soviet Union, Azerbaijan retained much antiquated equipment on its underground system.

underground rail systems in the West by the end of the 1970s. Azerbaijan, however, was a former Soviet republic and had retained much of its antiquated equipment because it was too poor to replace it.

Soon, the fire in the tunnel set light to the middle of the stranded train. The heat in the enclosed space was so intense that it quickly melted the doors and windows and those who had been travelling in the third carriage had virtually no chance of escape.

Eventually, some of the windows did get smashed and some of the doors were prised open – survivor Gennadi Nikiferev said that when this happened "people just fell out on top of each other." But those who did get out of the train alive were still not safe – by now, the killer fumes had spread about 200 yards (183m) further along the tunnel. And there was a hidden danger – although there had been a complete power failure at the scene of the disaster, electricity was still flowing through sections of the track closer to Narimanov station – some people who did not realize this were electrocuted. Even those who did struggle to safety along the track arrived choking and vomiting and were rushed to hospital to be treated for the effects of smoke inhalation.

Survivors told horrific tales of panic and screaming and the deaths of 28 children. Manish Gurbanov, who had been in the second carriage, said: "We could not break the windows so we climbed out through a ventilation duct. I got through the tunnel by grabbing a cable on the top. People were dying all over the rails."

Right: A survivor of the underground disaster is treated at the Baku Central Clinic.

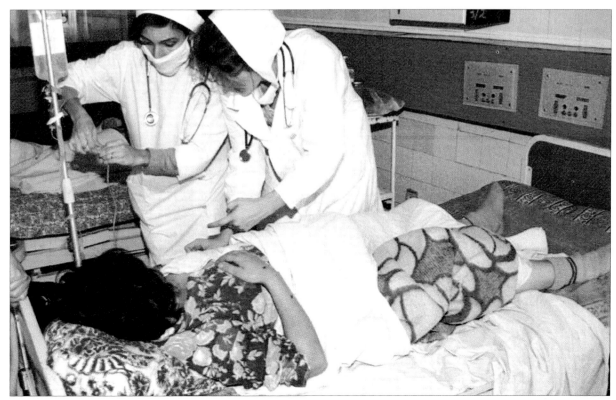

BROOKLYN SUBWAY, NEW YORK, USA

NOVEMBER 26, 1995

A New York subway clerk was badly injured when two youths lit a bottle of flammable liquid and threw it into his token booth at a station in Brooklyn, New York. The booth was destroyed and the clerk, Harry Kaufman, aged 50, suffered serious burns to 80 per cent of his body.

The following day, reports of the attack appeared in newspapers and on television and radio in many parts of the world. Despite the seriousness of the crime, it

would probably not have made international news had it not been for the similarities between it and a movie then on general release. *Money Train*, starring Wesley Snipes and Woody Harrelson, featured scenes – some of which were filmed in the New York subway system – in which a pyromaniac douses the insides of token booths with kerosene and then sets them alight.

Bob Dole, Republican leader of the Senate, who was then running for President of the USA, was quick to point out the link between screen violence and real-life

Above: Token booths for tickets on the New York subway. It was a token booth like this that was firebombed on November 26, 1995, badly injuring the clerk.

crime. He deplored "the pornography of violence to sell movie tickets" and said: "the American people have a right to voice their outrage . . . by derailing *Money Train* at the box office."

These views were supported by New York police commissioner William J. Bratton and Transit Authority President Alan F. Kiepper, who both said that the arson might have been inspired by the film. Meanwhile, Rudolph W. Giuliani, Mayor of New York, reacted defensively to hostile criticism of raising money by charging film makers to do location shooting. He told reporters: "The city should not be reading every script and acting as a censor."

Columbia Pictures, which produced the $60 million thriller, took a completely different view of the bombing. They issued a statement saying that they were "appalled and dismayed" by the attack. However, they denied that it was a copycat crime, claiming that the script had been based on a series of similar incidents in the early 1980s: they said that the fire had been art imitating life, rather than the other way round. As one executive put it: "We didn't invent this."

All token booths on the New York subway system are equipped with fire sensors which, when triggered either automatically or manually, emit halon from a canister to snuff out the fire and send an emergency signal to a command center. On the night of the arson, the sensors in Mr Kaufman's booth at Kingston-Throop Avenue station had been disabled just before the attack. Some people thought that this might have been because the clerk wanted to smoke a cigarette at his desk, but the Transport Workers' Union representatives thought this sounded like an attempt to muddy the waters and smear Mr Kaufman: "I'm wondering if the Transit Authority do all the maintenance work they should on these units," said a spokesman. "Why don't we look into that?"

Far right: The entrance to a New York subway station.

Below: A scene from the film Money Train. *The film featured a scene in which an arsonist set light to a New York token booth.*

INDUSTRIAL FIRES

Some of the most catastrophic fire disasters have been caused by industry. Two of the cases discussed in this chapter involve lorries with flammable or combustible cargoes crashing into human habitations. They both caused multiple deaths and considerable damage, but they are nevertheless fairly easy to grasp – industrial fires of the simplest sort.

But the consequences of other industrial fires are so wide-ranging as to be incalculable. In 1986, there was a fairly small fire at a chemical plant near Basel, Switzerland. It was soon brought under control and no one was burned or asphyxiated, but that was not the end of the story. The water used to spray the flames became contaminated with toxic chemicals and was then drained into the River Rhine. The poison spread over such a large area that it will never be known exactly how much damage was caused, although some environmentalists believe it may have been one of the greatest disasters in European history.

The 1997 bush fires in Indonesia – which were started deliberately by the owners of forests and plantations – soon created a persistent smog across a large part of southeast Asia and threatened a number of already endangered species of wildlife. The most disturbing aspect of this inferno was that it quickly reached the point at which it could no longer be extinguished by humans – it could only be left to burn itself out or be damped down by the monsoon.

If the human species is going to destroy itself or the planet Earth, the weapon it is most likely to use is fire.

Right: When a gas main fractured and caught fire in Ukhta, Russia, it caused an inferno that was so fierce local people fled from their homes, thinking war had broken out.

TRIANGLE WAIST FACTORY, NEW YORK, USA

MARCH 24, 1911

One hundred and forty-six workers were killed when fire swept through a shirt factory on the top three floors of a 10-storey building at the corner of Greene Street and Washington Place in New York City. Some 125 of the victims were young women aged between 16 and 23.

The Triangle Waist Company – the name of the firm referred to the idealized shape of the male torso when wearing one of its shirts – was a sweatshop in a squalid loft building. The tragedy highlighted the plight of blue collar workers who were exploited by having to put in long hours for poor pay in dangerous conditions.

The fire broke out on the eighth floor at 1640 hours, five minutes before closing time as the workers were getting ready to go home. During the week there would normally have been many more people in the building, but it was Saturday and only the Triangle staff – 700 of them, including 600 women – were working because the owners had a rush job on. Most of the women were Germans, Hungarians, Italians, and Russians, recent immigrants who had been hired after the firm had fired nearly all their old workers – most of whom were Jewish – when they became unionized and demanded better working conditions. At about the same time, the building – which had had four previous fires recently –

Below: The Triangle Waist Factory building had 10 storeys and was classified as fireproof by the New York City authorities.

Above: The scene inside the garment factory after fire swept through the top floors where women were working on a rush job on a Saturday afternoon.

Right: One of the elevators after the fire. The other elevator was not working.

had been reported to the authorities because of the inadequacy of its exits. However, no action had been taken to improve them.

The flames spread rapidly through the flimsy material on the racks and the offcuts which were piled high on the floor beside the machines. Some of the victims burned or were suffocated by fumes; others leaped 100 feet (30m) to their death down the lift shafts or from upstairs windows – many bodies were found in the street clutching their pay envelopes. The fire brigade tried to catch some of the jumpers in firenets – sheets held outstretched like trampolines by at least three people – but their efforts were futile: one girl jumped and landed safely, but three others followed her down and landed on the same net before she could get off. All four were killed by the impact.

Nevertheless, many other people jumped whom the fire brigade believed they might have saved. One girl who saw the glass roof of a sidewalk cover at the first floor level of the nearby New York University building leaped for it: her aim was right, but she crashed through it onto the sidewalk. Another girl waved a handkerchief as she jumped – about half way down she

Above: Firemen searching for bodies after the fire. Many women jumped to their deaths from the top floors of the building where they were trapped.

got her dress caught on a wire sticking out of the side of the building. The crowd watched helplessly as she hung there until her dress burned free and she fell to her death on the road.

The emergency services were so busy dealing with the fire that they could do no more than pile up dead bodies in the street. Then someone noticed that among them was a girl who was still breathing – they pulled her out at once, but she died two minutes later.

The structure of the building had been classed as fireproof by the New York City authorities. Although its exterior emerged virtually undamaged, inside the building the top three floors were completely gutted in less than half an hour. There was only one fire escape, and that was internal.

Two of Triangle Waist's owners, Isaac Harris and Max Blanck, were in the building at the time of the fire but escaped over the roof. This was an exit unknown to the staff who had always used the two freight elevators, one of which was not working on the afternoon of the fire. Police investigators subsequently discovered that two of the girls who had died, who were working on the ninth floor, had been locked into their work room. US labor law had strict rules forbidding employers to lock or bolt in their workers.

The Triangle Waist fire and its causes were important in the growth of the US trade union movement. Previously, clothing unions had struggled to attract new members because workers were too worried about keeping their jobs to agitate for better pay and conditions. This fire drew public attention to the plight of people in sweatshops; and in reaction against the fire, large numbers of garment workers now joined labor collectives.

FLIXBOROUGH, ENGLAND

JUNE 1, 1974

Above: The explosion at the Nypro works near Flixborough was the worst explosion in Britain since World War II. The region was declared a disaster area.

In the world's worst disaster in the chemical industry, 29 workers were killed and more than 40 injured when fire caused by an explosion gutted the £18 million ($29 million) Nypro nylon works at Flixborough, near Scunthorpe, Lincolnshire. Hundreds of acres of surrounding countryside were devastated by the resulting conflagration.

The Flixborough plant – which was owned jointly by the British National Coal Board (NCB) and Dutch State Mines – was at the time the main source of material for most British man-made textiles. It was used principally to make caprolactam, an essential component in the manufacture of nylon fibres. This material is obtained from cyclohexane, which in turn is a byproduct of coal-coking processes: it is highly flammable and has general properties similar to those of gasoline.

The seat of the explosion in the 20-acre (8 hectares) factory was an area known as Section 8 – it was here that the cyclohexane was oxidized by being heated and subjected to intense pressure. Nearly all the victims were working inside Section 8 or in the immediate vicinity – the dead were thought to have been killed instantly by a sudden surge of intense heat.

The disaster took place late on a Saturday night, when only 70 people were working in the entire plant. If the explosion had happened during a normal working weekday, the death toll would almost certainly have been much higher: Flixborough normally had 200 people on duty in every shift from Monday morning through to Friday evening.

Twenty-four hours after the explosion, a pall of smoke rising from the ruins of the factory was still visible more than 20 miles (32km) away. For days, emergency services could not actually extinguish the fire, which went on for almost a week before exhausting itself, rather than being extinguished. There was for a time a grave fear of radioactive fallout from a container of gamma-ray material that was known to be in the plant, but once the fire began to subside the canister was discovered intact in one of the less badly affected parts of the factory.

As the full scale of the disaster became clearer, it was discovered that the blast had been so great that it had rocked the foundations of houses in the village of Amcotte on the other side of the River Trent. Even at that distance from the explosion, serious structural damage had been caused to a number of substantial buildings: the pillars of the church were shaken, and the church was closed pending a full structural survey.

Water that had been used by the fire brigade to douse the flames lay in lagoons in the surrounding fields and was later found to be seriously contaminated with toxic chemical waste. Much of this liquid was eventually drained into the River Trent, only 100 yards (90m) from the plant: this led to serious pollution and threatened local wildlife.

Above: *A cloud of toxic smoke hides the remains of the chemical factory that exploded on June 1, 1974, killing 29 people.*

Right: *People from 100 houses near the factory were evacuated because their homes had been damaged by the blast.*

SAN CARLOS DE LA RAPITA, SPAIN

JULY 11, 1978

Above: The scene at the Los Alfraques camp site in Spain after a tanker carrying liquid propylene crashed on to the site and exploded, devastating the area and killing almost 200 campers.

Nearly 200 vacationers – most of them French or German and many of them children – were killed when a tanker truck with a cargo of liquid gas caught fire and then exploded after crashing into a crowded camp site on the Mediterranean coast of Spain.

It was about 1515 hours on a hot summer's afternoon when a truck hit a cement wall on the coast road at San Carlos de la Rapita, about 100 miles (160km) north of Valencia and 120 miles (192km) south of Barcelona. The driver lost control and his vehicle careered off the coast road and plunged down a hillside into the Los Alfraques camp site.

The truck, owned by the Cisternas Reunidas company, was believed to have been traveling along this slow, twisting route only in order to avoid paying the 1000 peseta toll on the turnpike which had recently been built to bypass this whole tourist seaside area.

Its tank was full almost to capacity with propylene – a gas used in the manufacture of alcohol and transported in the form of a pressurized liquid. Although it is highly inflammable, propylene is supposed not to be explosive. This puzzled crash investigators until eyewitnesses reported that they had seen flames coming from the truck before it went out of control – the propylene had evidently been heated by the fire on board for some time before it exploded.

The force of the blast was so great that it left a crater 20 yards (18m) across and hurled some of the campers 100 yards (90m) into the sea. It completely destroyed tents, a discothèque, and 12 holiday chalets. It also set off a chain of minor explosions in the bottled gas used by campers and the gasoline tanks of cars.

Right: A burned-out caravan on the camp site. The explosion completely destroyed tents and caravans, plus 12 chalets and a discothèque.

The death toll was high because at the time of the crash most of the campers were cleaning up after lunch or taking their siesta. If the accident had happened earlier in the day the death toll would almost certainly have been lower, because most people at the camp site would still have been swimming or sunbathing on the nearby beach.

Volunteers at the scene of the disaster said that identification of the bodies was virtually impossible because the explosion had dismembered them and the flames charred them beyond recognition. Nearly everyone was wearing swimsuits, which concealed little and protected even less flesh, so that most of the injured had extensive burns to between 50 and 90 percent of their bodies. The response to the disaster was immediate. The Spanish government put Air Force aircraft and helicopters at the disposal of the local authorities to evacuate the most serious cases. Cars and buses were commandeered to take the injured to clinics and hospitals all along the coast. Radio stations broadcast emergency appeals for blood donors.

So many of the injured were from Germany that the German government made arrangements the same day to airlift doctors and medical equipment to Spain from Stuttgart. Other nationalities among the victims included Belgian, British, and Dutch.

Right: Many of the campers were taking their afternoon siesta when the truck careered into their midst and exploded. Some were killed outright while others were hurled by the blast into the sea.

SANDOZ FACTORY, BASEL, SWITZERLAND

NOVEMBER 1, 1986

A relatively small fire in a chemical factory on the banks of the River Rhine near Basel, Switzerland, resulted indirectly in one of the most serious cases of environmental pollution the world has ever seen.

The incident occurred at the Schweizerhalle works of Sandoz, the Swiss chemical manufacturing conglomerate. Fire broke out in Warehouse 956, an open-plan hall measuring 295 by 164 feet (90 by 50m) and 32 feet (10m) from floor to ceiling.

Here, a consignment of Prussian blue artists' pigment was loaded onto a palette and then shrinkwrapped by heating plastic sheets with a blow torch. The flames were supposed to be kept at a distance of at least 12 inches (30cm) from the plastic, but it is believed that the torch may have been held too close, and the package overheated. This almost certainly happened during the day shift, but Prussian blue may glow smokelessly for up to 12 hours before it ignites. It was not until 0019 hours that a night worker first noticed a fire. At almost exactly the same time, a Basel police traffic patrol spotted flames shooting from the roof of the warehouse and alerted the fire brigade. The works' fire crew arrived at 0022 and within minutes they were joined by back-up teams from Basel and a fireboat on the Rhine. Within the hour, 160 firemen were in action at the scene.

The fire was put out shortly before 0500 hours and the firemen then turned their attention to cooling down the smoking ruins. But by this time large quantities of toxic chemicals had already been released in the form of smoke – these included carbon monoxide, sulphur, phosphorus, nitrogen, and carbon.

Worst of all was dioxin, a lethal by-product of the manufacture of herbicides which – under its other name, Agent Orange – was used as a defoliant in the Vietnam War.

Below: When fire broke out in the Sandoz chemical factory in Basel it released large quantities of toxic fumes into the atmosphere.

Right: Firemen extinguishing the last of the fire in the factory. An enormous volume of water was used to put out the fire, and this water subsequently drained into the Rhine river, polluting it with many poisons.

Below: One of the divers employed to clean up the Rhine is scrubbed clean after surfacing. Large vacuum hoses were used to suck up the contaminated mud at the bottom of the river.

Within days, the Rhine had turned an intense red color. This was at first attributed to the dyes that had been stored in Warehouse 956, but it later became apparent that about 3.3 million gallons (15,000 cubic meters) of water used to douse the flames had been contaminated with insecticides before being drained into the river via the sewer network. The poison spread downstream, and eventually more than 155 miles (250km) of the Rhine suffered severe ecological damage and many forms of wildlife were affected.

Because of fears about the poison being communicated to humans through the food chain, both the Swiss and German governments immediately banned all fishing in the Rhine. Thousands of square yards (meters) of the river bottom were then cleaned by the removal of the upper layer of silt with electrosuction equipment – more than 2200 lbs (1000kg) of toxic waste were recovered in this way. Although the Rhine was declared safe on July 1, 1987, the Sandoz company faced claims for compensation amounting to 100 million Swiss francs. In addition to numerous individual claimants, compensation was also sought by several German cities downstream of the disaster.

GASOLINE TANKER, HERBORN, GERMANY

JULY 7, 1987

A fully loaded gasoline tanker smashed into a busy ice-cream parlor in the German town of Herborn, killing 50 people and injuring a further 25. Fuel leaked from the truck and spread right across the town center – as a result, when the gasoline caught light a couple of minutes later, the whole place was quickly turned into a firebomb. In the immediate aftermath of the disaster, the municipal authorities declared a state of emergency and evacuated 20,000 nearby flats and houses. Although most people were allowed back into their homes five hours later, those who lived closest to the blast had to be accommodated overnight in local schools.

The tanker, which was carrying 7000 gallons (32,000 liters) of gasoline, had left the nearby Frankfurt-Ruhr autobahn with overheated brakes shortly before it crashed into the building housing an ice-cream parlor and pizza restaurant at about 2050 hours. The death toll might have been much greater, had it not been for the fact that the pizza restaurant was closed.

The tanker caught fire on impact with the wall. Many of the dead were trapped inside the restaurant, which was quickly razed to the ground. A little later, the flames set off gas pipeline explosions in eight adjacent houses, three of which were completely destroyed. Ambulances, fire engines, police, and rescue services raced to the scene. After tending to the

Below: When a tanker went out of control and crashed into an ice-cream parlor the resulting explosion set off a fire that affected most of the center of Herborn.

Above: After the initial impact, gas explosions in adjoining houses caused further devastation.

most seriously injured, their main concern was the possibility of further explosions. Gasoline from the tanker had flooded into the underground sewage system and the surrounding air was thick with inflammable and toxic fumes: almost any part of Herborn was now a potential inferno.

Meanwhile, the roads into the town had become blocked by hundreds of cars full of ghoulish sightseers who had come to look at the scene of carnage. As a result, precious time was lost while helicopter ambulances were scrambled to airlift the injured to hospital. Amazingly, the tanker driver himself was only slightly hurt. This was because he had had enough time after the impact and before the explosion to jump out of his cab. The time lag between the crash and the explosion was confirmed by bystanders. One, Roger

Schmidt, described how he had rushed into the street after hearing the tanker smash into the corner of the building. "A couple of minutes later, there was a massive blast," he said. "I think the water in the sewage system exploded with the gasoline that had poured into it. Manhole covers flew into the air."

Another eyewitness, Hagen Puthner, aged 18, reported that he had heard the blast from his home where he had been having a meal with a friend. "There were flames and the earth was burning. People were crying for help. We tried to get a ladder but the flames were too high."

'There is hardly a brick left standing where the restaurant was," said a police spokesman, "It is a catastrophe. There have never been so many deaths here before. We are not used to this."

PIPER ALPHA OIL RIG, NORTH SEA

JULY 6, 1988

A huge fire caused by two explosions on Piper Alpha, an offshore oil drilling rig in the North Sea about 120 miles east of Wick, Scotland, killed 151 men. Flames from the inferno leaped more than 200 feet (60m) into the air.

On the evening of Wednesday, July 6, 1988, the Aberdeen coast guard received a mayday call from the *Lowland Cavalier*, an oil rig support vessel in the North Sea. The message – "Explosion on the Piper Alpha" – was logged at 2158 hours.

The explosion had happened at 2131 hours, and the rescue teams were immediately puzzled why there had been such a long delay before the distress call had been put out. It was only when they reached the rig and

saw the extent of the devastation that they realized: there had been too much panic even to call for help.

Over the next two hours, there was a massive response by the British emergency services. Twelve RAF helicopters, a Nimrod search and rescue maritime patrol aircraft, six Royal Navy warships, a fisheries protection vessel, and an assortment of oil rig and coast guard vessels and commercial helicopters all made full speed to the scene of the disaster. The NATO Standing Naval Force Atlantic also became involved: this was a unique aspect of the operation.

In the minutes after the first blast, the men on board the rig itself had to make a fateful decision: whether to remain on the platform and wait for help to arrive, or to jump 40 feet (12m) into the water below, which was

Above: Two days after the explosion that claimed 151 lives, the Piper Alpha oil rig was still belching black smoke. In the background is a fire fighting platform.

119

seething close to boiling point. The 70 men who survived this disaster all took their chance and threw themselves upon the mercy of the sea.

The first ship to sight the blazing platform was the *Tharos*. This support vessel – which had been patrolling nearby – had hospital accommodation for 22 as well as fire-fighting equipment. But before it could come within range of the stricken rig, a second explosion tore away the remains of the platform and killed anyone who had not already jumped overboard. The crew of the *Tharos* could do no more than watch as oilmen waved frantically for help from the helipad before the final blast – in the words of one onlooker – "just blew them away".

The *Tharos* picked the first survivors out of the water at 2210 hours, but further efforts to help were hampered by the intensity of the blaze, which forced the vessel to pull back a mile (1.6km) from the platform. The injured received emergency treatment on board the rescue ship.

The exact cause of the disaster was never conclusively established. One theory was that the explosions occurred after a sudden surge of gas escaped from a pocket in the reservoir beneath the North Sea oil bed. This might have been ignited by a chance spark on the platform. Survivors spoke of the squealing sound of escaping gas about 30 seconds before the first explosion: "a screaming like a banshee", as one of them described it.

In the aftermath of the tragedy, Piper Alpha was declared a safety hazard and was sunk. The Piper field, however, later resumed full production.

Below: About 70 percent of the Piper Alpha rig was destroyed by the explosion and fire. A diver support vessel lies close by as the rig still smolders.

GAS PIPELINE, UKHTA, RUSSIA

APRIL 27, 1995

A fireball from a fractured Russian gas pipeline leaped thousands of feet into the air and burned for more than two hours after a spark had ignited a leak from the 55-inch (140-cm) main pipe. The flames were so fierce that some local residents fled from their homes, believing that war had broken out.

The incident happened near Ukhta, an oil-refining centre 800 miles (1300km) northeast of Moscow in the semi-autonomous Komi Republic. Intense heat kept firefighters more than half a mile (0.8 km) at bay for

over two hours. The blaze forced a Japanese Airlines flight to alter course as it cruised at 31,000 feet (9300m) en route from Frankfurt to Tokyo. The pilot of the Boeing 747, Akira Yamakawa, reported: "I saw a red burning cloud below at one moment and then it became black. That was repeated again and again. We didn't know what was happening. We felt very uneasy."

Despite the ferocity of the conflagration, Russian officials said that no one had been killed or even injured. Indeed, they were at pains to play down the significance of the event – a government spokesman described it as "an ordinary fire" and added "there is no

Above: The fire from the fractured gas main was so fierce that firefighters could not get near it, and a Japanese airliner had to alter course even though it was cruising high above it.

need to worry." But the Tass news agency later admitted: "The Russian side routinely informed the US about the incident," presumably to allay any fears that it might have been a nuclear test.

The pipeline forms part of a 137,000 mile (219,000 km) network operated by RAO Gazprom, the Russian national gas monopoly. The lines are a constant source of concern to environmentalists all over the world because they frequently leak gas into the atmosphere. They are also liable to crack or rupture at almost any time, especially in the extreme cold of a Siberian winter. The network was built during the Soviet era and, although the pipes are made of high-grade iron imported from Germany, the PVC coating with which they are covered is only about one third of the ⅛-inch (3mm) standard thickness to which pipelines in Europe and the US are required to conform. The welded pipeline seams are also highly vulnerable. Losses to the atmosphere from Russian pipelines are thought to exceed 10 percent every year – this is at least 10 times the level acceptable in the West.

The Ukhta explosion was almost certainly a great fire disaster, albeit one about which the full truth will probably never be known. Even if the Russian version of events is accurate, the same type of explosion might happen again, almost anywhere in the country.

Below: Smoke continued to pour from the fractured gas main in Ukhta, even after the blaze had been brought under control.

TAEGU GAS EXPLOSION, SOUTH KOREA

APRIL 28, 1995

I n one of South Korea's worst peacetime disasters, at least 110 people – including 60 teenagers and 10 children – were killed by a horrific gas explosion beneath a busy road in Taegu, a city with a population of 2.2 million, 150 miles south of the capital, Seoul. More than 200 others were seriously injured.

The tragedy took place at a main intersection at about 0730 hours in the morning as heavy rush hour traffic sat in lines waiting their turn to go through the lights. An underground railway was being built directly beneath one of the roads at the crossing, and the normal tarmac highway had been replaced with metal sheets as a temporary surface while the excavations were carried out.

Below: At the scene of devastation following the gas explosion rescue workers search for victims.

Eyewitnesses said that when the blast came, it shook the surrounding area like an earthquake and the metal road sheets were blown high into the air by a great jet of flame. Ten houses and public buildings in the immediate vicinity of the intersection were completely destroyed in an instant; a little further away, another 60 were badly damaged.

Thirty vehicles were engulfed by flames at once, while another 30 fell over 30 feet (9m) through the temporary paving onto the underground construction site. Other buses, cars, and trucks were hurled through the air like confetti.

A vast fireball erupted from below the ground, killing rush hour commuters and children crossing the road on their way to school. The jet of flame eventually reached more than 150 feet (45m) into the air above a 300-yard (274m) stretch of mangled highway. The fire consumed everything in its path and, as it did so, it turned into a pall of choking black smoke.

Huge chunks of metal were thrown high into the air, and as they came back to earth over an area about a quarter of a mile (0.4km) wide, pedestrians who had not been harmed by the initial blast were killed when they were hit by lumps of debris the size of office desks. Many of the most seriously injured were pinned to the ground by metallic objects which had dropped on them from out of the sky.

One survivor, Park Yoon Ho, a 17-year-old student, heard a loud explosion on his way to school. "Then I was blown down by a gust that sent out a mushroom of dust," he said. "It looked like the explosion of an atomic bomb on television."

The disaster is thought to have been caused either when one of the tunneling drills fractured a gas pipe or when a spark from some other electrical tool ignited an existing leak.

The emergency services attempting to save the construction workers trapped underground were hampered by fractured water mains, which gushed forth sheets of water, flooding the railway construction pit and making it difficult to work. The explosion also cut off the electricity supplies and so firefighters and ambulance men had to use their own mobile emergency generators. About 4000 soldiers, police, and firemen took part in the operation which went on all through the following night.

Left: After the explosion many building workers were trapped in the underground railway construction site. Here a South Korean policeman uses a rope to lift a wounded man out of the site.

BUSH FIRES, INDONESIA
1997

For most of 1997, up to a million hectares of forest, scrubland, and plantation burned out of control across much of Sumatra and Kalimantan (the Indonesian part of the island of Borneo). This was one of the most wide-ranging fires ever and presented an enormous ongoing threat, not only to the many rare and endangered species of wildlife in its path, but also to the whole ecosystem of the planet Earth.

The logging industry is Indonesia's second largest revenue earner after oil and gas, and the government of that country is anxious to expand its palm oil, wood pulp, and rubber industries by replacing its natural forests with plantations. It plans to develop 4.4 million hectares of pulp plantations for timber by the year 2004, and 5.5 million hectares of palm oil plantations by 2000. The simplest way to clear existing forests is by setting fire to them. So these fires were started delib-erately by the owners of forests and plantations – even though it has been illegal to do so since 1994.

Because of these fires, Indonesia's natural forest cover has decreased from 80 percent of the total land area in the 1960s to 57 percent today. Environmentalists fear that, if the present rate of depredation continues, the nation's forests will have been entirely laid waste by 2030.

Logged forest is more susceptible to fire than unlogged forest – this is partly because of the debris left on the ground, and partly because logging opens up the tree canopy, allowing more sunlight to enter and dry the forest floor. Moreover, much of the forest floor is made up of peat and this, combined with burning underground root systems, makes the fires much harder to control.

The smoke from these fires combined with pollutants from cities in Indonesia and Malaysia to create a suffocating smog that blocked out the sun and caused

Above:
Indonesian servicemen manhandle a hose to help a Malaysian fireman tackle the forest fires in central Sumatra. The smog resulting from the extensive fires caused severe breathing difficulties in many people in the region.

serious breathing problems to populations throughout the region. The smog contained particles of burnt vegetation suspended in the air. The smoke itself was made up of numerous toxic chemicals including sulphur dioxide, hydrogen sulphide, nitrogen oxide, carbon monoxide, and ammonia.

The smog spread on the wind as far as Singapore, the Philippines, and southern Thailand and stayed in these regions even after the fires which caused them had burnt themselves out: up to 70 million people are thought to have been affected.

The 1997 Indonesian forest fires were not without precedent. In 1982-3, for example, an area of East Kalimantan about the size of Belgium (13,000 square miles/33,000 sq km) was destroyed by flames. The effects were lasting – one of the most striking is the persistent haze, which has become an annual summer feature of the weather in this part of the world.

The 1997 forest fires were made worse by El Niño, an unusual drought-inducing weather phenomenon which normally occurs once every two to seven years. Normally, the fires would have been put out by the monsoon in early autumn. In 1997 there was a severe

Above: Fire-fighters battle with the forest fires in Indonesia in October 1997.

Left: Despite the gas masks worn by these Malaysian firemen, one man had to be evacuated when the dense smog brought on an asthma attack.

Left: As the forest fires continue out of control, villagers in central Sumatra protect an oil pipeline supplying southern Sumatra by throwing buckets of river water over it.

drought in southeast Asia and the fires burnt on uncontrolled right through the autumn months.

This area is rich in endangered wildlife, and among the species threatened by the conflagration were the Sumatran tiger (of which there are only 400 to 500 left), the Javan rhinoceros (about 100 to 200) and the orangutan (about 30,000).

One of the greatest fears is that these fires will contribute significantly to world climate changes through the emission of massive amounts of carbon monoxide. This is a matter of grave concern to many other nations because of the greenhouse effect which reduces the oxygen supply and may shortly threaten all forms of life on Earth.

In a conference on greenhouse gas emissions in Washington, DC, in October 1997, US President Bill Clinton expressed his nation's grave concern about events in southeast Asia. "If we expect other nations to tackle the problem," he said, "then we must show them leadership." Unfortunately, there is as yet no international agreement about exactly what form this leadership should take. Japan, for example, believes that a reduction of 5 percent on 1990 emission levels by 2012 is sufficient to save the planet. By contrast, the European Union believes that target is inadequate and has called for a 15 per cent reduction even sooner – no later than 2010.

Above: Indonesian soldiers and Malaysian firefighters pick up their equipment as they come to the end of a logging railway line that has been partially destroyed by the bush fires. Many of the thousands of firefighters had to battle their way through the jungle to reach the fires they were trying to put out.

INDEX

Abadan, *August 19, 1978* 38–9
Afghanistan, Salang Pass Tunnel, *November 2 or 3, 1982* 8, 41–2
Alcalà 20 disco, *December 17, 1983* 98–9
Alexandra Palace, *July 10, 1980* 74–5
arson 26–7, 40, 48–9, 104–5
   Kuwait oil fields 45–7
   terrorism 38–9
Ash Wednesday bush fires, *February 16, 1983* 12, 28–9
Atlanta, Winecoff Hotel, *December 7, 1946* 59
Australia *see* Ash Wednesday bush fires
Azerbaijan *see* Baku

Baku, subway train, *October 29, 1995* 102–3
Basel, Sandoz factory, *November 1, 1986* 9, 106, 115–16
Belgium *see* Brussels
Berlin
   Loebel Cafe, *February 8, 1947* 60
   Reichstag fire, *February 27, 1933* 12, 26–7
bombing raids 32–5
Boston, Cocoanut Grove Club, *November 28, 1942* 57–8
Bradford City football stadium, *May 11, 1985* 8, 82–3
Brazil *see* Sao Paolo
Brooklyn subway, *November 26, 1995* 104–5
Brussels, L'Innovation, *May 22, 1967* 63–4
bush fires 11, 12, 28–9, 106

camp sites 113–14
Charles II, King of England 17
chemical plants 9, 106, 111–12, 115–16
Chicago
   Great Fire of Chicago, *October 8-10, 1871* 6, 12, 20–1
   Iroquois Theater, *December 30, 1903* 52–3
   Our Lady of the Angels School, *December 1, 1958* 61–2
Chile *see* Santiago
churches 12, 18–19, 54
cinemas 38, 78–9
Club Cinq-Sept, *November 1, 1970* 65–6
clubs/night clubs/discos 40, 65, 67–8, 73, 98–9
Cocoanut Grove Club, *November 28, 1942* 57–8
Costesti Church, *April 18, 1930* 54
Crystal Palace, *November 30, 1936* 55–6

department stores 63–4, 67–8
der Lubbe, Marinus van 26, 27
discos/clubs/night clubs 40, 65, 67–8, 73, 98–9
Dresden, *February 13-17, 1945* 34–5

Düsseldorf Airport, *April 11, 1996* 88–9

earthquakes, causing fires 7, 22–5
England *see* Bradford City football stadium; Flixborough; Hampton Court Palace; London; Man, Isle of; Windsor Castle; York

factories *see* Flixborough; Sandoz factory; Triangle Waist factory
fire exits 8–11
firebombing
   gasoline/petrol 38, 40
   incendiary devices 7, 33, 36
firestorms 32, 34–5, 36
Flixborough, *June 1, 1974* 111–12
football stadia 8, 82–3
forest fires *see* bush fires
France *see* Grenoble

gas pipelines 10, 106, 121–2
Germany *see* Berlin; Düsseldorf Airport; Hamburg; Herborn
Göring, Hermann 27
Grand Hotel, *November 21, 1980* 76–7
Great Fire of Chicago, *October 8-10, 1871* 6, 12, 20–1
Great Fire of London, *September 2-5, 1666* 16–17
Great Fire of Rome, *July 18, AD 64* 14–15
Grenoble, Club Cinq-Sept, *November 1, 1970* 7, 65–6

Hamburg, *July 25-28, 1943* 32–3
Hampton Court Palace, *March 31, 1986* 9, 50, 84–5
Herborn, *July 7, 1987* 117–18
Hitler, Adolf 26–7
hotels 59, 73, 76–7

Idaho, Kellogg mine, *May 2, 1972* 96–7
incendiary devices (firebombing) 7, 33, 36
Indonesia, bush fires, *1997* 11, 106, 125–7
industrial fires 106–27
Iran, Abadan, *August 19, 1978* 38–9
Iroquois Theater, *December 30, 1903* 52–3
Isle of Man, Summerland Leisure Center, *August 2, 1973* 69–70
Italy *see* Rome; Turin; Venice

Japan *see* Osaka; Tokyo; Yokohama
Joelma Building, *February 1, 1974* 7, 71–2

Kellogg mine, *May 2, 1972* 96–7
King's Cross Underground station, *November 18, 1987* 11, 90, 100–1
Kuwait, oil fields, *February-November, 1991* 45–7

La Compania Church, *December 8, 1863* 12, 18–19
La Fenice theater, *January 30, 1996* 11, 30, 48–9
Las Vegas, Grand Hotel, *November 21, 1980* 76–7
lightning 80
L'Innovation, *May 22, 1967* 63–4
Loebel Cafe, *February 8, 1947* 60
London
   Alexandra Palace, *July 10, 1980* 74–5
   Crystal Palace, *November 30, 1936* 55–6
   Great Fire of London, *September 2-5, 1666* 16–17
   King's Cross Underground station, *November 18, 1987* 11, 90, 100–1
   Rodo's and El Hueco's Clubs, *August 16, 1980* 40

Madrid, Alcalà 20 disco, *December 17, 1983* 98–9
Mafia 49
Man, Isle of, *1973* 7
mines 11, 92–7
Money Train (movie) 104–5
Move fire 8, 43–4

Nero, Emperor 14, 15
New York
   Brooklyn subway, *November 26, 1995* 104–5
   Triangle Waist factory, *March 24, 1911* 11, 108–10
night clubs/clubs/discos 40, 65, 67–8, 73, 98–9
North Sea, Piper Alpha oil rig, *July 6, 1988* 11, 119–20

oil fields, Kuwaiti, *February-November, 1991* 45–7
oil rigs 11, 119–20
"Operation Gomorrah" 32
Osaka, Sennichi building, *May 13, 1972* 67–8
Our Lady of the Angels School, *December 1, 1958* 61–2

Pepys, Samuel 16
Philadelphia, the Move fire, *May 15, 1985* 8, 43–4
Piper Alpha oil rig, *July 6, 1988* 11, 119–20
public places 8–11, 40, 50–89

Romania, Costesti Church, *April 18, 1930* 54
Rome, *July 18, AD 64* 14–15
Roosevelt, Franklin D. 7
Russia *see* Ukhta

Salang Pass Tunnel, *November 2 or 3, 1982* 8, 41–2

San Carlos de la Rapita, *July 11, 1978* 113–14
San Francisco, *April 18-21, 1906* 7
Sandoz factory, *November 1, 1986* 9, 106, 115–16
Santiago, La Compania Church, *December 8, 1863* 12, 18–19
Sao Paolo, Joelma Building, *February 1, 1974* 7, 71–2
schools 61–2
Sengenhydd mine, *October 14, 1913* 92–3
Sennichi building, *May 13, 1972* 67–8
Seoul, hotel fire, *November 3, 1974* 73
South Korea *see* Seoul; Taegu
Spain *see* Madrid; San Carlos de la Rapita
Statuto Cinema, *February 13, 1983* 78–9
Summerland Leisure Center, *August 2, 1973* 69–70

Taegu, gas explosion, *April 28, 1995* 123–4
tankers, gasoline 117–18
terrorism *see* arson
theaters *see* cinemas; Iroquois Theater; La Fenice theater
Thompson, John "Gypsy" 7, 40
Tokyo
   March 9-10, 1945 7, 36–7
   September 2, 1923 24–5
Triangle Waist factory, *March 24, 1911* 11, 108–10
Turin, Statuto Cinema, *February 13, 1983* 78–9

Ukhta, gas pipeline, *April 27, 1995* 10, 106, 121–2
underground fires 11, 90–105
USA *see* Atlanta; Boston; Chicago; Idaho; Las Vegas; New York; Philadelphia; San Francisco; West Virginia

Venice, La Fenice theater, *January 30, 1996* 11, 30, 48–9

Wales, Sengenhydd mine, *October 14, 1913* 92–3
wars *see* Afghanistan; World War II
West Virginia, mine near Farmington, *November 20, 1968* 94–5
Windsor Castle, *November 20, 1992* 86–7
Winecoff Hotel, *December 7, 1946* 59
World War II
   Dresden, *February 13-17, 1945* 34–5
   Hamburg, *July 25-28, 1943* 32–3
   Tokyo, *March 9-10, 1945* 7, 36–7
Wren, Christopher 17, 84

Yokohama, *September 2, 1923* 24–5
York, York Minster, *July 9, 1984* 80–1